Verse by Verse Commentary on the Book of

2 SAMUEL

Enduring Word Commentary Series

By David Guzik

The grass withers, the flower fades,
but the word of our God stands forever.
Isaiah 40:8

Commentary on 2 Samuel

Copyright ©2019 by David Guzik

Printed in the United States of America
or in the United Kingdom

Print Edition ISBN: 1-56599-038-2

Enduring Word

5662 Calle Real #184

Goleta, CA 93117

Electronic Mail: ewm@enduringword.com

Internet Home Page: www.enduringword.com

Scripture references, unless noted, are from the New King James Version of the Bible, copyright ©1979, 1980, 1982, Thomas Nelson, Inc., Publisher.

Contents

*To Richard and Eleanor -
Father and Mother
to their own David*

2 Samuel 1 - David Mourns the Death of Saul

A. David learns of Saul and Jonathan's deaths.

1. (1-4) David hears the news in Ziklag.

Now it came to pass after the death of Saul, when David had returned from the slaughter of the Amalekites, and David had stayed two days in Ziklag, on the third day, behold, it happened that a man came from Saul's camp with his clothes torn and dust on his head. So it was, when he came to David, that he fell to the ground and prostrated himself. And David said to him, "Where have you come from?" So he said to him, "I have escaped from the camp of Israel." Then David said to him, "How did the matter go? Please tell me." And he answered, "The people have fled from the battle, many of the people are fallen and dead, and Saul and Jonathan his son are dead also."

> a. **After the death of Saul**: King Saul and his three sons were killed in battle against the Philistines, dying on the slopes of Mount Gilboa (1 Samuel 31:1-8). It was the sad ending of a tragic life, concluding the story of a man who came to the throne humble but left it hardened, bitter against both God and man.

> b. **When David returned from the slaughter of the Amalekites**: Towards the end of 1 Samuel, despairing David left the people of God and allied himself with the Philistines. God prevented a complete alliance and brought David back through heartbreaking circumstances (the **Amalekites** stole the families and possessions of David and his men). Strengthening himself in God (1 Samuel 30:6), David defeated the **Amalekites** and brought back everyone and everything.

> > i. Though David still lived among the Philistines, he was a changed man since his heartbreaking circumstances and since strengthening himself in the LORD.

ii. When David came back triumphantly to Ziklag, he knew a battle between the Philistines and the Israelites just ended. He certainly was concerned about the outcome of that battle.

c. **A man came from Saul's camp with his clothes torn and dust on his head**: David knew this was bad news because the messenger had the traditional expressions of mourning for the dead - **clothes torn and dust on his head**. Therefore, he immediately reacted with humble mourning

2. (5-10) The Amalekite's story.

So David said to the young man who told him, "How do you know that Saul and Jonathan his son are dead?" Then the young man who told him said, "As I happened by chance *to be* on Mount Gilboa, there was Saul, leaning on his spear; and indeed the chariots and horsemen followed hard after him. Now when he looked behind him, he saw me and called to me. And I answered, 'Here I am.' And he said to me, 'Who *are* you?' So I answered him, 'I *am* an Amalekite.' He said to me again, 'Please stand over me and kill me, for anguish has come upon me, but my life still *remains* in me.' So I stood over him and killed him, because I was sure that he could not live after he had fallen. And I took the crown that *was* on his head and the bracelet that *was* on his arm, and have brought them here to my lord."

a. **As I happened by chance to be on Mount Gilboa**: Some wonder if this Amalekite told the truth. He said he "mercifully" ended Saul's life after the king mortally wounded himself (1 Samuel 31:4). It may be that he merely was the first to come upon Saul's dead body and he took the royal **crown** and **bracelet** to receive a reward from David.

i. "The whole account which this young man gives is a fabrication: in many of the particulars it is grossly *self-contradictory*. There is no *fact* in the case but the bringing of the *crown*, or *diadem*, and *bracelets* of Saul; which, as he appears to have been a plunderer of the slain, he found on the field of battle; and he brought them to David, and told the lie of having dispatched Saul merely to ingratiate himself with David." (Clarke)

ii. We can gather that this was a lie because 1 Samuel 31:5 says that Saul's armor bearer saw that he was dead.

b. **I am an Amalekite**: If we do take the Amalekite's story as true, this is a chilling statement. In a unique war of judgment, God commanded Saul to completely destroy the people of Amalek (1 Samuel 15:2-3). Saul failed to do this - and **an Amalekite** brought a bitter end to his tragic life.

i. Though the Bible does not specifically say it, Amalek is commonly regarded as an illustration of our fleshly, carnal nature.

- Like our fleshly nature, Amalek focuses its attack on the tired and weak (Deuteronomy 25:17-18).

- Like our fleshly nature, Amalek does not fear God (Deuteronomy 25:17-18).

- Like our fleshly nature, God commanded a permanent state of war against Amalek (Exodus 17:16).

- Like our fleshly nature, the battle against Amalek is only won in the context of prayer and seeking God (Exodus 17:11).

- Like our fleshly nature, God promises to one day completely blot out the remembrance of Amalek (Exodus 17:14).

- Like our fleshly nature, Joshua wins the battle against Amalek (Exodus 17:13).

- Like our fleshly nature, Amalek was once first but will one day be last (Numbers 24:20).

- Like our fleshly nature, Amalek allies itself with other enemies in battle against God's people (Judges 3:13).

ii. Using this picture, we see that Saul's failure to deal with Amalek when God told him to resulted in ruin, with an Amalekite delivering the death-blow. In the same way, when we fail to deal with the flesh as God prompts us, we can expect that area of the flesh to come back and deliver some deadly strikes.

c. **I took the crown that was on his head and the bracelet that was on his arm, and have brought them here to my lord**: We can easily imagine the Amalekite smiling as he said this, assuming David was delighted that his enemy and rival was dead. *Now* David could take the royal **crown** and **bracelet** and wear them himself.

3. (11-12) David's reaction: mourning for Saul.

Therefore **David took hold of his own clothes and tore them, and** *so did* **all the men who** *were* **with him. And they mourned and wept and fasted until evening for Saul and for Jonathan his son, for the people of the** Lord **and for the house of Israel, because they had fallen by the sword.**

a. **David took hold of his own clothes and tore them**: When David heard of Saul's death, *he mourned*. We might have expected *celebration* at the death of this great enemy and rival, but David **mourned**.

i. Out of pure jealousy, hatred, spite, and ungodliness, Saul took away David's family, home, career, security, and the best years of David's life - and Saul was *utterly unrepentant* to the end. Yet David **mourned and wept and fasted** when he learned of Saul's death.

ii. This contrast powerfully demonstrates that our hatred, bitterness, and unforgiveness are *chosen*, not *imposed* on us. As much as Saul did against David, he chose to become *better* instead of *bitter*.

b. **And so did all the men who were with him**: These men had their own reasons to hate Saul, but they followed the example of their leader, David, and answered Saul's hatred and venom with love.

c. **For Saul and Jonathan... for the people of the LORD and for the house of Israel**: David's sorrow was first for Saul, but it was also for his great and close friend Jonathan. More than that, it was for the people of God as a whole, who were in a dangerous and desperate place in light of the death of the king and the defeat by the Philistines.

i. David heard this life-changing news - the throne of Israel was now vacant, and it seemed that the royal anointing he received some 20 years before might now be fulfilled with the crown set on his head. Nevertheless, David expressed little thought of himself. "His generous soul, oblivious to itself, poured out a flood of the noblest tears man ever shed for Saul, and for Jonathan his son, and for the people of the Lord, and for the house of Israel, because they were fallen by the sword." (Meyer)

4. (13-16) David executes the Amalekite.

Then David said to the young man who told him, "Where *are* you from?" And he answered, "I *am* the son of an alien, an Amalekite." So David said to him, "How was it you were not afraid to put forth your hand to destroy the LORD's anointed?" Then David called one of the young men and said, "Go near, *and* execute him!" And he struck him so that he died. So David said to him, "Your blood *is* on your own head, for your own mouth has testified against you, saying, 'I have killed the LORD's anointed.'"

a. **Where are you from**: The young Amalekite probably believed that David was preparing to reward him.

b. **How was it you were not afraid to put forth your hand to destroy the LORD's anointed**: Despite many opportunities to legitimately defend himself, David refused to reach out and destroy Saul. David knew that since God put Saul on the throne, it was God's job to end his reign - and woe to the one who puts forth *his* hand to destroy a God-appointed leader.

c. **Go near, and execute him**: This shows that David's grief over Saul was real. He didn't put on a false display of grief and then secretly honor the man who killed Saul.

d. **Your blood is on your own head, for your own mouth has testified against you**: There were many factors that might excuse what the Amalekite did and said.

- Saul was in rebellion and hardened against God.
- Saul repeatedly and constantly tried to kill David.
- Saul was already near death.
- Saul asked the Amalekite to kill him.
- It may be that the Amalekite merely discovered Saul's dead body.

    i. Yet none of these excuses mattered. Except for justified killing in war, self-defense, or lawful criminal execution, it is God's job to end a life - not ours. This is true of every human life, but it is even truer of the life and ministry of **the LORD's anointed** - God is fully able to deal with His servants, even those who only *claim* to be His servants.

B. David's lament for Saul and Jonathan

1. (17-18) Introduction to the **Song of the Bow**.

Then David lamented with this lamentation over Saul and over Jonathan his son, and he told *them* **to teach the children of Judah** *the Song of* **the Bow; indeed** *it is* **written in the Book of Jasher:**

a. **David lamented with this lamentation**: David's sorrow was sincere and deeply felt. He crafted a song to express the depth of his feeling.

b. **The book of Jashar**: This book is also mentioned in Joshua 10:13; it evidently contained a collection of early Hebrew poetry.

    i. We shouldn't think that this is a "missing" book of the Bible. It is a *completely unjustified leap* over logic to say that if the Bible *mentions* an ancient writing, and if that ancient writing has any material in common with Biblical books, that writing is genuinely Scripture and is a "lost" book of the Bible. Our Bibles are complete and completely inspired.

2. (19-27) The **Song of the Bow**.

"The beauty of Israel is slain on your high places!
How the mighty have fallen!
Tell *it* **not in Gath,**
Proclaim *it* **not in the streets of Ashkelon;**
Lest the daughters of the Philistines rejoice,

Lest the daughters of the uncircumcised triumph.
O mountains of Gilboa,
Let there be no dew nor rain upon you,
Nor fields of offerings.
For the shield of the mighty is cast away there!
The shield of Saul, not anointed with oil.
From the blood of the slain,
From the fat of the mighty,
The bow of Jonathan did not turn back,
And the sword of Saul did not return empty.
Saul and Jonathan *were* beloved and pleasant in their lives,
And in their death they were not divided;
They were swifter than eagles,
They were stronger than lions.
O daughters of Israel, weep over Saul,
Who clothed you in scarlet, with luxury;
Who put ornaments of gold on your apparel.
How the mighty have fallen in the midst of the battle!
Jonathan *was* slain in your high places.
I am distressed for you, my brother Jonathan;
You have been very pleasant to me;
Your love to me was wonderful,
Surpassing the love of women.
How the mighty have fallen,
And the weapons of war perished!"

a. **The beauty of Israel is slain**: In this song, David showed the great love and generosity in his heart towards Saul. It showed that David didn't kill Saul with a sword or in his heart.

- He saw **beauty** in Saul.

- He wanted no one to **rejoice** over the death of Saul.

- He wanted everyone to mourn, even the **mountains** and **fields**.

- He praised Saul as a **mighty** warrior.

- He complimented the personality and loyalty of Saul (**not divided**).

- He called the **daughters Israel** to mourning and praised the good Saul did for Israel.

    i. All this is a powerful testimony of how David kept his heart free from bitterness, even when he was greatly wronged and sinned against. David fulfilled 1 Corinthians 13:5: *love thinks no evil*. David knew the principle of 1 Peter 4:8: *And above all things have fervent love for one another, for "love will cover a multitude of sins."*

ii. David could do this because of his great trust in God and God's power. He knew that God was in charge of his life, and that even if Saul meant it for evil, God could use it for good.

iii. "Such a magnanimous attitude on the part of one who had suffered so much at Saul's hand is incomprehensible apart from a deep commitment to the Lord." (Baldwin)

b. **How the mighty have fallen**: David doesn't say it, but we understand that Saul *fell* long before this. He fell when he hardened his heart against God, against the word of God through the prophet, and against the man after God's own heart. Saul's death on Gilboa was the sad conclusion to his prior fall.

c. **I am distressed for you, my brother Jonathan**: David's mourning for Jonathan makes more sense to us. Jonathan was David's deep friend and partner in serving God.

i. **Your love to me was wonderful, surpassing the love of women**: Had David followed God's plan for marriage - to one woman, faithful for a lifetime - he might have found more fulfillment in his marriage relationship. We remember that David's own experience of love with women was not according to God's will. His multiple marriages kept him from God's ideal: one man and one woman in a one-flesh relationship.

ii. There is not the slightest hint that David and Jonathan expressed their love in a sexual way. They had a deep, godly love for each other - but not a sexual love. Our modern age often finds it difficult to believe that love can be deep and real without it having a sexual aspect.

2 Samuel 2 - David and the War with Ishbosheth

A. Two kings over the people of God.

1. (1-4a) David, king of Judah.

It happened after this that David inquired of the LORD, saying, "Shall I go up to any of the cities of Judah?" And the LORD said to him, "Go up." David said, "Where shall I go up?" And He said, "To Hebron." So David went up there, and his two wives also, Ahinoam the Jezreelitess, and Abigail the widow of Nabal the Carmelite. And David brought up the men who *were* with him, every man with his household. So they dwelt in the cities of Hebron. Then the men of Judah came, and there they anointed David king over the house of Judah.

a. **David inquired of the LORD**: Certainly, this was a key to success in David's life. With rare exceptions, he constantly **inquired of the LORD**. David wanted more than God's blessing on *his* plans; he wanted to be right in the middle of *God's* plan.

b. **Shall I go up to any of the cities of Judah**: At this time David was still in Ziklag, in the territory of the Philistines. Out of great discouragement and despair, he left the land of Israel and lived almost as a Philistine among the Philistines. Now that David was restored to the LORD, he wondered if it was time for him to go back to his homeland.

i. It isn't as simple a question as we might think. David didn't want to appear opportunistic, as if he *only* came back to Israel because Saul was dead. While not being *overly* concerned with appearances before man, he was not *unconcerned* with appearances either.

c. **And the LORD said to him**: God was faithful to answer when David inquired. Since David just came out of a period of spiritual decline, God could have put him on "probation" and refused to speak to him for a while. Instead, the LORD spoke to David and gave him guidance.

17

i. Some 15 to 20 years before this, David was anointed king over Israel (1 Samuel 16:12-13). As the promise seems almost fulfilled, David didn't rush in blindly and seize it. Instead, he carefully sought the LORD. David knew the promise was from God, so he knew God could fulfill it without any manipulation from David.

d. **There they anointed David king**: This shows that David did not seize the throne. The elders of Judah approached him. David knew that it was better to let God lift you up through others than to strive to advance yourself. We should strive to advance God's Kingdom and leave the advancement of self in His hands.

i. This also shows that there is a sense in which the first anointing wasn't enough. We need a fresh anointing from God and ongoing experience with the Holy Spirit.

ii. This anointing couldn't come when David still lived among the Philistines virtually as a Philistine. He had to get things right in his own walk before this fresh anointing.

2. (4b-7) David thanks the men of Jabesh Gilead.

And they told David, saying, "The men of Jabesh Gilead *were the ones* who buried Saul." So David sent messengers to the men of Jabesh Gilead, and said to them, "You *are* blessed of the LORD, for you have shown this kindness to your lord, to Saul, and have buried him. And now may the LORD show kindness and truth to you. I also will repay you this kindness, because you have done this thing. Now therefore, let your hands be strengthened, and be valiant; for your master Saul is dead, and also the house of Judah has anointed me king over them."

a. **You have shown this kindness to your lord, to Saul, and have buried him**: David showed appropriate gratitude to the men who risked their lives to honor the memory of Saul and Jonathan (1 Samuel 31:11-13).

b. **Let your hands be strengthened, and be valiant**: David knew that he needed brave men like these to secure and advance his kingdom, especially in the turmoil sure to surround his ascension to the throne.

3. (8-11) Abner sets up Ishbosheth as king over Israel.

But Abner the son of Ner, commander of Saul's army, took Ishbosheth the son of Saul and brought him over to Mahanaim; and he made him king over Gilead, over the Ashurites, over Jezreel, over Ephraim, over Benjamin, and over all Israel. Ishbosheth, Saul's son, *was* forty years old when he began to reign over Israel, and he reigned two years. Only the house of Judah followed David. And the time that David was king in Hebron over the house of Judah was seven years and six months.

a. **Abner the son of Ner**: Abner was Saul's cousin (1 Samuel 14:50) and the commander of Saul's armies for many years. He first met David when David was a young man (1 Samuel 17:55-57). David once challenged Abner when he had the opportunity to kill Saul but did not. David pointed out that Abner failed to protect his king.

b. **Ishbosheth the Son of Saul**: Saul had three sons who died with him in battle (1 Samuel 31:6). There is no previous mention of **Ishbosheth** among the sons of Saul, so it is possible that he was an illegitimate son or the son of a concubine.

> i. We shouldn't forget that David was also a son of Saul by marriage. David married Michal, the daughter of Saul (1 Samuel 18:17-30).

c. **He made him king**: Abner **made** Ishbosheth king, probably so that he could be the real power behind the throne of a weak king.

d. **He reigned two years**: For **two years** David allowed Ishbosheth to reign over most of Israel. These two years showed remarkable patience, longsuffering, and trust in God on David's part. Ishbosheth was not the Lord's anointed like Saul - David seemed to have every right to crush this man who stood in the way of his calling. Yet out of trust in the Lord and respect for Saul's memory, David waited.

> i. It seems strange that many of the tribes preferred Ishbosheth to David. Yet since the Philistines had overrun many of the other tribes of Israel, they were even more hesitant to come out-and-out for David. "We'll just make the Philistines mad," they thought. In the same way, if you will come out-and-out for the Son of David, you have to be ready for the disapproval of the Philistines.

e. **Seven years and six months**: This describes the period of time David had his headquarters in Hebron. For the first two years of this time, he ruled over Judah alone and Ishbosheth (propped up by Abner) ruled the rest of Israel.

> i. David refused to force his reign on his subjects - and neither will the Son of David. Like David, Jesus will battle against pretenders to the throne, but He will not force His reign on mankind - yet.

B. War between the tribe of Judah and the other tribes of Israel.

1. (12-17) Abner's troops and Joab's troops square off and fiercely battle.

Now Abner the son of Ner, and the servants of Ishbosheth the son of Saul, went out from Mahanaim to Gibeon. And Joab the son of Zeruiah, and the servants of David, went out and met them by the pool of Gibeon. So they sat down, one on one side of the pool and the other on the other

side of the pool. Then Abner said to Joab, "Let the young men now arise and compete before us." And Joab said, "Let them arise." So they arose and went over by number, twelve from Benjamin, *followers* of Ishbosheth the son of Saul, and twelve from the servants of David. And each one grasped his opponent by the head and *thrust* his sword in his opponent's side; so they fell down together. Therefore that place was called the Field of Sharp Swords, which *is* in Gibeon. So there was a very fierce battle that day, and Abner and the men of Israel were beaten before the servants of David.

a. **Joab the son of Zeruiah**: Joab was apparently one of the 400 men who joined David at Adullam Cave (1 Samuel 22:1-2), or he joined with David during this general period.

- Joab had two notable brothers: Abishai and Asahel.

- Joab, Abishai, and Asahel were David's nephews, the sons of David's sister Zeruiah (1 Chronicles 2:16).

- Joab had a long and checkered career as David's chief general.

b. **Abner said to Joab**: This was a fascinating confrontation between two similar men. **Abner** and **Joab** were each tough, mean, military men who were completely devoted to their cause.

c. **Let the young men now arise and compete before us**: Abner suggested some kind of contest or duel between a select group of his men and Joab's men. When the two groups of 12 met, it quickly degenerated into a mutual bloodbath (**each one grasped his opponent by the head and thrust his sword in his opponent's side; so they fell down together**). Yet David's men under the command of Joab prevailed in the **very fierce battle** that followed this bloodbath at **the Field of Sharp Swords**.

i. "This was diabolical play, where each man thrust his sword into the body of the other, so that the twenty-four (twelve on each side) fell down dead together!" (Clarke)

2. (18-23) Abner kills Asahel.

Now the three sons of Zeruiah were there: Joab and Abishai and Asahel. And Asahel *was as* fleet of foot as a wild gazelle. So Asahel pursued Abner, and in going he did not turn to the right hand or to the left from following Abner. Then Abner looked behind him and said, *"Are* you Asahel?" He answered, "I *am.*" And Abner said to him, "Turn aside to your right hand or to your left, and lay hold on one of the young men and take his armor for yourself." But Asahel would not turn aside from following him. So Abner said again to Asahel, "Turn aside from following me. Why should I strike you to the ground? How then could I

face your brother Joab?" However, he refused to turn aside. Therefore
Abner struck him in the stomach with the blunt end of the spear, so that
the spear came out of his back; and he fell down there and died on the
spot. So it was *that* as many as came to the place where Asahel fell down
and died, stood still.

a. **The three sons of Zeruiah**: Zeruiah was David's sister (1 Chronicles
2:16). **Joab and Abishai and Asahel** were the nephews of David, but since
David was the youngest of eight sons, they may have been about the same
age or older than David.

b. **Asahel pursued Abner**: In the pressure and confusion of battle, Asahel
got close enough to Abner, the commander of Ishbosheth's armies. It came
down to a simple chase, and if Asahel caught up to Abner, he would surely
kill him.

c. **Lay hold of one of the young men and take his armor for yourself**:
It seems that Asahel pursued Abner in part for the glory of killing the
commander of Ishbosheth's army and taking **his armor** as a trophy.

d. **Why should I strike you to the ground? How then could I face your
brother Joab**: Abner first asked Asahel to turn back out of concern for his
own safety. This didn't make much sense to Asahel because it seemed that
Abner was at the disadvantage. Abner also appealed to Asahel on the ground
of military honor - that officers should not strike down officers, especially
when it might lead to ugly retribution and the danger of leaderless armies.

i. Yet, Asahel **refused to turn aside**. Abner's plea didn't work -
though perhaps it should have. Asahel was too single-minded in his
determination to kill Abner and crush the armies opposing David.

e. **Therefore Abner struck him in the stomach... he fell down there and
died on the spot**: Clearly, Abner killed Asahel in self-defense - it was the
only thing he could do. Yet his concern (**How then could I face your
brother Joab**) was entirely justified, and Joab will make it his passion to
avenge his brother's death.

3. (24-28) A cease-fire called.

**Joab and Abishai also pursued Abner. And the sun was going down
when they came to the hill of Ammah, which *is* before Giah by the road
to the Wilderness of Gibeon. Now the children of Benjamin gathered
together behind Abner and became a unit, and took their stand on top
of a hill. Then Abner called to Joab and said, "Shall the sword devour
forever? Do you not know that it will be bitter in the latter end? How
long will it be then until you tell the people to return from pursuing
their brethren?" And Joab said, "*As* God lives, unless you had spoken,**

surely then by morning all the people would have given up pursuing their brethren." So Joab blew a trumpet; and all the people stood still and did not pursue Israel anymore, nor did they fight anymore.

a. **Joab and Abishai also pursued Abner**: Now more than the cause of David motivated them. They wanted to avenge the killing of their brother Asahel.

b. **Shall the sword devour forever**: When his armies were in full retreat and ready for a final do-or-die stand - and when two angry brothers wanted blood revenge - Joab found it easy to make the plea for peace. It was certainly to his advantage to give peace a chance.

c. **Joab blew a trumpet; and all the people stood still**: Joab agreed to this cease-fire, probably to both rest his exhausted army and to of avoid a long, bloody civil war.

4. (2:29-3:1) A great victory for David's army.

Then Abner and his men went on all that night through the plain, crossed over the Jordan, and went through all Bithron; and they came to Mahanaim. So Joab returned from pursuing Abner. And when he had gathered all the people together, there were missing of David's servants nineteen men and Asahel. But the servants of David had struck down, of Benjamin and Abner's men, three hundred and sixty men who died. Then they took up Asahel and buried him in his father's tomb, which *was in* Bethlehem. And Joab and his men went all night, and they came to Hebron at daybreak. Now there was a long war between the house of Saul and the house of David. But David grew stronger and stronger, and the house of Saul grew weaker and weaker.

a. **There were missing of David's servants nineteen men and Asahel**: 2 Samuel 2:17 told us *Abner and the men of Israel were beaten before the servants of David*, but this passage shows us just how badly they were beaten. Abner and the army of Ishbosheth lost 360 men to 20 in the army of David.

b. **There was a long war between the house of Saul and the house of David**: This shows how wrong it was for Joab to accept Abner's appeal for a cease-fire at the battle of The Field of Sharp Swords. The fact was that they *couldn't* just get along, and that there could be no peace between the rightful king David and the pretender to the throne, Ishbosheth. The cease-fire seemed to make things better, but in reality, it only made things worse and it led to the **long war**.

i. When we try to make peace between King Jesus and King Self within us, the result is a long, bitter war. It is so much better to simply surrender and submit to the reign of Jesus.

ii. "In the lives of many Christian people today there is raging, literally, a civil war. The flesh - the kingdom of Saul, struggles with the spirit - the kingdom of David, and the conflict is bitter. We do everything we possibly can to hold up the tottering kingdom of self, so that it might exist just a bit longer. If only we could preserve some rights; if only we could have at least part of our own way; if only we could keep this or that at any cost! We feel we must bolster up this kingdom of self, that we cannot let ourselves be crucified with Christ." (Redpath)

c. **David grew stronger and stronger**: The increasing strength of David and increasing weakness of Saul's house did not begin when Saul died. It began when God first chose David and withdrew His Spirit from Saul (1 Samuel 16:13-14).

2 Samuel 3 - Abner's Defection and Murder

A. Abner defects from Ishbosheth.

1. (2-5) David's sons born in Hebron.

Sons were born to David in Hebron: His firstborn was Amnon by Ahinoam the Jezreelitess; his second, Chileab, by Abigail the widow of Nabal the Carmelite; the third, Absalom the son of Maacah, the daughter of Talmai, king of Geshur; the fourth, Adonijah the son of Haggith; the fifth, Shephatiah the son of Abital; and the sixth, Ithream, by David's wife Eglah. These were born to David in Hebron.

> a. **Sons were born to David**: During David's seven-year reign in Hebron, his six different wives gave birth to six sons. This shows that David went against God's commandment that Israel's king should not multiply wives to himself.
>
> > i. David was *wrong* to have more than one wife. His many wives went against God's command to kings (Deuteronomy 17:17) and against God's heart for marriage (Genesis 2:24, Matthew 19:4-6).
> >
> > ii. David's many wives were *common*. Adding many wives was one way great men and especially kings expressed their power and status.
> >
> > iii. David was *troubled* because of his many wives. Some wonder why the Bible doesn't expressly condemn David's polygamy here, but as is often the case, the Scripture simply states the fact and later records how David reaped the penalty for this sort of sin in regard to his family.
>
> b. **These were born to David in Hebron**: We must say that God used and blessed David *despite* his many wives. Yet his family life and these sons were obviously not blessed. "By six wives he had but six sons. God was not pleased with his polygamy." (Trapp)
>
> > i. **Amnon** raped his half-sister and was murdered by his half-brother.

ii. **Chileab** is also known as *Daniel* in 1 Chronicles 3:1. The few mentions of this son indicate that perhaps he died young or that he was an ungodly, unworthy man.

iii. **Absalom** murdered his half-brother and led a civil war against his father David, attempting to murder David.

iv. **Adonijah** tried to seize the throne from David and David's appointed successor - then he tried to take one of David's concubines and was executed for his arrogance.

v. We can fairly assume that **Shephatiah** and **Ithream** either died young or were ungodly and unworthy men because they are mentioned only once again in the Scriptures - in a generic listing of David's sons (1 Chronicles 3:1-4).

2. (6-7) Ishbosheth accuses Abner of impropriety with the royal concubine.

Now it was so, while there was war between the house of Saul and the house of David, that Abner was strengthening *his hold* on the house of Saul. And Saul had a concubine, whose name *was* Rizpah, the daughter of Aiah. So *Ishbosheth* said to Abner, "Why have you gone in to my father's concubine?"

a. **Abner was strengthening his hold on the house of Saul**: It seems that Abner supported a weak man like Ishbosheth in power, so he could be the power behind the throne. As time went on, he increased in strength and influence **on the house of Saul**.

b. **Why have you gone in to my father's concubine**: Ishbosheth accused Abner of a serious crime. Taking a royal **concubine** was regarded as both sexual immorality and treason.

i. "To take the wife or concubine of the late monarch was to appropriate his property and to make a bid for the throne." (Baldwin)

ii. This might seem strange that there was a controversy over the **concubine** of **Saul**, especially because Saul was dead. Yet in their thinking, the king's bride belonged to him and him alone, even if he was absent. This principle is even more true for Jesus and His bride - the church belongs to no one but Jesus, and it is treason to "take" the bride of Christ as if she were our own possession.

3. (8-11) Abner's harsh reply.

Then Abner became very angry at the words of Ishbosheth, and said, "*Am* I a dog's head that belongs to Judah? Today I show loyalty to the house of Saul your father, to his brothers, and to his friends, and have not delivered you into the hand of David; and you charge me today with

a fault concerning this woman? May God do so to Abner, and more also, if I do not do for David as the LORD has sworn to him—to transfer the kingdom from the house of Saul, and set up the throne of David over Israel and over Judah, from Dan to Beersheba." And he could not answer Abner another word, because he feared him.

a. **Then Abner became very angry**: We aren't specifically told, but Abner's response leads us to believe that the accusation was false. It is possible that as he *was strengthening his hold on the house of Saul* he took the concubine as an expression of his power and dominance. It is more likely that because of Abner's increasing power Ishbosheth felt it necessary to invent this accusation as a reason to get rid of Abner.

b. **If I do not do for David as the LORD has sworn to him**: Abner told Ishbosheth that he would now support David and help David fulfill what the LORD promised - **to transfer the kingdom from the house of Saul, and set up the throne of David**.

i. If Abner knew that David was God's choice for king, he had no good reason to fight against him before this. Abner is a good example of those of us who *know* things to be true, but we don't *live* as if they were true.

ii. Abner did the right thing in joining David's side, but he did it for the wrong reason. Instead of joining David because Ishbosheth offended him personally, he should have joined David because he knew that David was God's choice to be king.

4. (12-16) David agrees to receive Abner if he will bring Michal with him.

Then Abner sent messengers on his behalf to David, saying, "Whose *is* the land?" saying *also*, "Make your covenant with me, and indeed my hand *shall be* with you to bring all Israel to you." And *David* said, "Good, I will make a covenant with you. But one thing I require of you: you shall not see my face unless you first bring Michal, Saul's daughter, when you come to see my face." So David sent messengers to Ishbosheth, Saul's son, saying, "Give *me* my wife Michal, whom I betrothed to myself for a hundred foreskins of the Philistines." And Ishbosheth sent and took her from *her* husband, from Paltiel the son of Laish. Then her husband went along with her to Bahurim, weeping behind her. So Abner said to him, "Go, return!" And he returned.

a. **You shall not see my face unless you first bring Michal, Saul's daughter**: David received Michal in marriage (1 Samuel 18:26-28), but Saul took her away to spite David (1 Samuel 25:44).

b. **Whom I betrothed to myself with a hundred foreskins of the Philistines**: 1 Samuel 18:20-30 describes how David used this unusual payment instead of a dowry for the right to marry the daughter of King Saul.

> i. "He might have said two hundred; but he thought better to speak with the least." (Trapp)

c. **Give me my wife Michal**: Apparently, David was not done adding to his collection of wives. He insisted on receiving Michal as his wife again for at least three reasons.

> i. David remembered that Michal was his wife by both love and right and that King Saul took her away as part of a deliberate strategy to attack and destroy David.

> ii. David wanted to show that he harbored no bitterness towards Saul's house, and he would show this through his good treatment of Saul's daughter.

> iii. David wanted to give himself a greater claim to Saul's throne as his son-in-law.

> iv. "However distressing it was to take her from a husband who loved her most tenderly, yet prudence and policy required that he should strengthen his own interest in the kingdom as much as possible." (Clarke)

d. **Abner said to him, "Go, return!" And he returned**: This fits with the personality of Abner as we know him throughout 1 and 2 Samuel. Abner was a very tough guy.

5. (17-19) Abner rallies support for David among the other tribes.

Now Abner had communicated with the elders of Israel, saying, "In time past you were seeking for David *to be* king over you. Now then, do *it!* For the LORD has spoken of David, saying, 'By the hand of My servant David, I will save My people Israel from the hand of the Philistines and the hand of all their enemies.'" And Abner also spoke in the hearing of Benjamin. Then Abner also went to speak in the hearing of David in Hebron all that seemed good to Israel and the whole house of Benjamin.

a. **Abner had communicated with the elders of Israel**: It is significant that this word came from **Abner** regarding David instead of coming from David himself. Though he was the rightful king, David would not reign over Israel until they submitted to him freely. He never moved an inch without an invitation.

i. This is an illustration of Jesus' lordship in our life. He is in fact King of Kings and Lord of Lords. But He chooses (for the most part) to exercise His sovereignty only at our invitation.

- Some do not invite Jesus to rule over anything.
- Some invite Jesus to reign over a small area - like "Hebron."
- Some give Jesus reign over everything He has authority over - which is everything.

ii. Abner is a good example of someone who eventually surrendered to God's king. Now he wanted to influence others to also surrender to God's king.

b. **Now then, do it**: Because of the word the LORD spoke of David, and because it was so right to do, this was something that should be done **now**. In this sense, it is very much like our commitment to follow Jesus - we should be told, "**Now then, do it!**"

i. Charles Spurgeon has a wonderful sermon on this text titled, "Now Then, Do It." In this sermon he shows how the same principles of Israel's embrace of David as king apply to our relationship with Jesus. "The Israelites might talk about making David king, but they would not crown him. They might meet together and say they wished it were so, but that would not do it. It might be generally admitted that he ought to be monarch, and it might even be earnestly hoped that one day he would be so, but that would not do it; something more decided must be done." (Spurgeon)

ii. "The sooner it is done the better. Until the deed is done, remember you are undone; till Christ is accepted by you as king, till sin is hated and Jesus is trusted, you are under another king. Whatever you may think of it, the devil is your master."

c. **For the LORD has spoken of David**: The fact that Abner - who was a general, not a Bible scholar - knew these prophecies and the fact that he could ask the leaders of Israel to consider them means that these prophecies of David were widely known. Sadly, they were not widely obeyed - most of Israel was lukewarm and unenthusiastic in their embrace of David as king.

i. In this regard David prefigures his greater Son. Jesus fulfilled all manner of prophecy regarding the Messiah, yet He was rejected by all but a remnant of Israel.

ii. We don't have a Biblical record of this exact statement Abner said **the LORD has spoken of David**. "We read not that God had so said in express terms: but either Abner had heard of such a promise made at the anointing of David by Samuel, or else feigned it of his own head for his own ends." (Trapp)

6. (20-21) David formally receives Abner with a feast.

So Abner and twenty men with him came to David at Hebron. And David made a feast for Abner and the men who *were* **with him. Then Abner said to David, "I will arise and go, and gather all Israel to my lord the king, that they may make a covenant with you, and that you may reign over all that your heart desires." So David sent Abner away, and he went in peace.**

a. **David made a feast for Abner**: This was David showing himself wise and generous towards a former adversary. A lesser man would never forgive Abner for leading an army against God's king, but David was a great, wise, and generous man.

b. **That you may reign over all that your heart desires**: Abner wanted David's reign to be fully realized over the people of God.

B. Joab murders Abner.

1. (22-25) Joab learns that Abner has joined David's side.

At that moment the servants of David and Joab came from a raid and brought much spoil with them. But Abner *was* **not with David in Hebron, for he had sent him away, and he had gone in peace. When Joab and all the troops that** *were* **with him had come, they told Joab, saying, "Abner the son of Ner came to the king, and he sent him away, and he has gone in peace." Then Joab came to the king and said, "What have you done? Look, Abner came to you; why** *is* **it** *that* **you sent him away, and he has already gone? Surely you realize that Abner the son of Ner came to deceive you, to know your going out and your coming in, and to know all that you are doing."**

a. **Surely you realize that Abner the son of Ner came to deceive you**: Joab accused Abner of being a double agent for Ishbosheth. He was angry that David let Abner go without arresting or killing him.

b. **Surely you realize that Abner the son of Ner came to deceive you**: This was one of at least three reasons why Joab was not pleased that Abner had defected and joined David's side.

i. Joab feared Abner was a deceiver, a double agent working on behalf of Ishbosheth, the pretender king.

ii. Abner killed Joab's brother, and Joab was the *avenger of blood* for Asahel (as described in Numbers 35:9-28).

iii. As the chief general of the former King Saul, Abner had a lot of top-level military experience. Abner might take Joab's place as David's chief military assistant.

2. (26-27) Joab murders Abner.

And when Joab had gone from David's presence, he sent messengers after Abner, who brought him back from the well of Sirah. But David did not know *it*. Now when Abner had returned to Hebron, Joab took him aside in the gate to speak with him privately, and there stabbed him in the stomach, so that he died for the blood of Asahel his brother.

a. **Joab took him aside in the gate**: Joab carefully engineered this murder so that the killing was done *outside* the gate of Hebron. This was because Hebron was a city of refuge (Joshua 20:7), and it was against the law for Joab, as Asahel's blood avenger, to kill Abner *inside* the city.

b. **He died for the blood of Asahel his brother**: The careful plot to murder Abner outside the city of refuge made the murder all the darker. It showed Joab *knew* that Abner had a rightful claim of self-defense and was protected inside the city of Hebron, yet he killed him anyway.

i. Joab may have justified this by the thought, "I'm doing this to defend and honor my king." But our sin and treachery never honors our king. We must avoid the trap Spurgeon spoke of: "We may even deceive ourselves into the belief that we are honoring our Lord and Master when we are, all the while, bringing disgrace upon his name."

3. (28-30) David renounces Joab's evil murder of Abner.

Afterward, when David heard *it*, he said, "My kingdom and I *are* guiltless before the LORD forever of the blood of Abner the son of Ner. Let it rest on the head of Joab and on all his father's house; and let there never fail to be in the house of Joab one who has a discharge or is a leper, who leans on a staff or falls by the sword, or who lacks bread." So Joab and Abishai his brother killed Abner, because he had killed their brother Asahel at Gibeon in the battle.

a. **My kingdom and I are guiltless before the LORD**: David knew that he had nothing to do with this murder. Among other evils, this murder perpetrated by Joab set a bad precedent. It gave David's administration a reputation for brutality and made it harder for David to win the rest of Israel over to his side.

b. **Let it rest on the head of Joab**: David pronounced a severe curse against Joab, but he *did nothing* to correct Joab. Perhaps David was afraid to lose Joab as a general. His ability to kill without remorse showed he was not a nice man, but not necessarily a bad general.

4. (31-39) David leads the mourning for Abner.

Then David said to Joab and to all the people who were with him, "Tear your clothes, gird yourselves with sackcloth, and mourn for Abner." And King David followed the coffin. So they buried Abner in Hebron; and the king lifted up his voice and wept at the grave of Abner, and all the people wept. And the king sang *a lament* **over Abner and said:**

"Should Abner die as a fool dies?
Your hands were not bound
Nor your feet put into fetters;
As a man falls before wicked men, *so* **you fell."**

Then all the people wept over him again. And when all the people came to persuade David to eat food while it was still day, David took an oath, saying, "God do so to me, and more also, if I taste bread or anything else till the sun goes down!" Now all the people took note *of it,* **and it pleased them, since whatever the king did pleased all the people. For all the people and all Israel understood that day that it had not been the king's** *intent* **to kill Abner the son of Ner. Then the king said to his servants, "Do you not know that a prince and a great man has fallen this day in Israel? And I** *am* **weak today, though anointed king; and these men, the sons of Zeruiah,** *are* **too harsh for me. The LORD shall repay the evildoer according to his wickedness."**

a. **The king lifted up his voice and wept at the grave of Abner**: David did not want his kingdom established by violence. He wanted God to establish his kingdom and to punish his enemies. David still believed that *vengeance belongs to the Lord.*

b. **For all the people and all Israel understood that day that it had not been the king's intent to kill Abner**: This whole affair was a mess, but it would not be the first or the last mess of David's kingdom.

i. In some regard, "messes" like this are inevitable. Proverbs 14:4 states an important principle: *Where no oxen are, the trough is clean; but much increase comes by the strength of an ox.*

2 Samuel 4 - The Assassination of Ishbosheth

A. Ishbosheth is murdered.

1. (1-4) The weakened condition of the house of Saul.

When Saul's son heard that Abner had died in Hebron, he lost heart, and all Israel was troubled. Now Saul's son *had* two men *who were* captains of troops. The name of one *was* Baanah and the name of the other Rechab, the sons of Rimmon the Beerothite, of the children of Benjamin. (For Beeroth also was *part* of Benjamin, because the Beerothites fled to Gittaim and have been sojourners there until this day.) Jonathan, Saul's son, had a son *who was* lame in *his* feet. He was five years old when the news about Saul and Jonathan came from Jezreel; and his nurse took him up and fled. And it happened, as she made haste to flee, that he fell and became lame. His name *was* Mephibosheth.

a. **He lost heart**: When Ishbosheth heard that the man who put and propped him on the throne was dead, he knew that his day was almost over. He trusted in man to gain his position, so when the man was gone, he knew his position would be soon gone. Ishbosheth was weak because he trusted in man.

b. **His name was Mephibosheth**: This was the son of Jonathan, David's good friend who died with his father on the field of battle. Mephibosheth was the last male descendant of Saul with a strong legal claim to the throne of Saul. At this time he was only 12 years old - and he was **lame**.

i. **As she made haste to flee, that he fell and became lame**: Mephibosheth was weak because of circumstances beyond his control. He was weak because of his age and because of injury that came from the hand of another.

2. (5-7) Baanah and Rechab murder Ishbosheth.

Then the sons of Rimmon the Beerothite, Rechab and Baanah, set out and came at about the heat of the day to the house of Ishbosheth, who was lying on his bed at noon. And they came there, all the way into the house, *as though* to get wheat, and they stabbed him in the stomach. Then Rechab and Baanah his brother escaped. For when they came into the house, he was lying on his bed in his bedroom; then they struck him and killed him, beheaded him and took his head, and were all night escaping through the plain.

a. **They stabbed him in the stomach**: Ishbosheth didn't gain any real loyalty among his troops; they were only loyal to him when they thought he was strong and had a chance to keep the throne of Saul. When the weakness of Ishbosheth was exposed, **Rechab and Baanah** murdered him.

i. 2 Samuel 4:2 reminds us that **Rechab and Baanah** were *of the children of Benjamin*. This was the tribe that Saul's family came from. This means that it was fellow Benjaminites who murdered Ishbosheth.

ii. **Who was lying on his bed at noon**: The mid-day *siesta* wasn't unusual in that part of the world, but the absence of guards points to carelessness on the part of Ishbosheth. "To sleep at noon, and without a guard, speaketh him both sluggish and secure. He dieth therefore in his sloth, who had lived slothfully all his days." (Trapp)

b. **Beheaded him and took his head**: This was an important part of their plan, because they wanted to prove to David that they murdered his rival to the throne.

B. David executes Ishbosheth's assassins.

1. (8) Baanah and Rechab bring the head of Ishbosheth to David.

And they brought the head of Ishbosheth to David at Hebron, and said to the king, "Here is the head of Ishbosheth, the son of Saul your enemy, who sought your life; and the LORD has avenged my lord the king this day of Saul and his descendants."

a. **And the LORD has avenged my lord the king this day of Saul and his descendants**: When they brought Ishbosheth's severed head to David they said, "We are God's servants, defeating your enemies as instruments of God."

i. "Their claim, *The Lord has avenged my lord the king*, was presuming on God's approval of their deed, as though they had acted on the Lord's express orders." (Baldwin)

b. **The son of Saul your enemy**: David couldn't relate to this because he didn't think of Saul as his **enemy**. The beautiful song David composed at the death of Saul and Jonathan proved that though Saul set himself as an enemy of David, David did not regard him as an **enemy**.

2. (9-12) David has Baanah and Rechab executed.

But David answered Rechab and Baanah his brother, the sons of Rimmon the Beerothite, and said to them, "As the LORD lives, who has redeemed my life from all adversity, when someone told me, saying, 'Look, Saul is dead,' thinking to have brought good news, I arrested him and had him executed in Ziklag—the one who *thought* I would give him a reward for *his* news. How much more, when wicked men have killed a righteous person in his own house on his bed? Therefore, shall I not now require his blood at your hand and remove you from the earth?" So David commanded his young men, and they executed them, cut off their hands and feet, and hanged *them* by the pool in Hebron. But they took the head of Ishbosheth and buried *it* in the tomb of Abner in Hebron.

a. **Shall I not now require his blood at your hand and remove you from the earth**: Rechab and Baanah thought David would be *pleased* to see the severed head of Ishbosheth. They underestimated David's loyalty to God and the house of Saul. David was loyal to his pledge to honor and preserve Saul's family and descendants (1 Samuel 24:20-22).

i. David was used to seeing severed heads - he carried the head of Goliath around as a trophy for some period of time. But David knew that Saul and his descendants were not his enemy the same way that Goliath was his enemy.

ii. Even though Ishbosheth was not *the* LORD's anointed in the same sense as Saul was, David had thoroughly learned to let *God* take vengeance.

iii. David would not accept their evil deed, even though it seemed to serve a good purpose - unifying Israel under David's reign as king. "While it is true that God overrules all the doings of men, and compels them ultimately to serve His high purposes, it is equally true that no servant of His can ever consent to do evil that good may come. It is an arresting truth that our Lord in the days of his earthly life would not accept the testimony of demons." (Morgan)

b. **David commanded his young men, and they executed them**: David swiftly made an example of these murderous men. They were not soldiers fighting together with him; they were murderers who deserved just punishment.

i. "By this act of justice, David showed to all Israel that he was a decided enemy to the destruction of Saul's family; and that none could lift up their hands against any of them without meeting with condign punishment." (Clarke)

ii. "Thus David acted with strict justice in this case also, not only to prove to the people that he had neither commanded nor approved of the murder, but from heartfelt abhorrence of such crimes, and to keep his conscience void of offense towards God and towards man." (Keil and Delitzsch)

2 Samuel 5 - David Made King Over A United Israel

A. David reigns over all Israel.

1. (1-3) The elders of Israel recognize David as king over Israel.

Then all the tribes of Israel came to David at Hebron and spoke, saying, "Indeed we *are* your bone and your flesh. Also, in time past, when Saul was king over us, you were the one who led Israel out and brought them in; and the LORD said to you, 'You shall shepherd My people Israel, and be ruler over Israel.'" Therefore all the elders of Israel came to the king at Hebron, and King David made a covenant with them at Hebron before the LORD. And they anointed David king over Israel.

> a. **Then all the tribes of Israel came to David**: Prior to this, only one of the tribes of Israel recognized David as king. The other tribes recognized the pretend king Ishbosheth, a son of Saul. Ishbosheth was murdered as recorded in 2 Samuel 4 - so now the tribes turned to David.
>
> > i. It's sad that the tribes only turned to David when their previous choice was taken away. On the same principle, it's sad when Christians only really recognized Jesus as king when other choices crumble. We should choose Jesus outright, not just when other options fail.
>
> b. **We are your bone and your flesh**: The elders of Israel received David's leadership because he was an Israelite himself. This was significant because for a period of time David lived as a Philistine among the Philistines. The elders of Israel put that away and embraced David as one of their own.
>
> c. **You were the one who led Israel out and brought them in**: The elders of Israel received David's leadership because he already displayed his ability to lead.

d. **The LORD said to you, "You shall shepherd My people Israel, and be ruler over Israel"**: The elders of Israel received David's leadership because it was evident God called him to lead.

> i. These three characteristics should mark anyone who leads God's people.
>
> • A leader must belong to God's people in heritage and heart.
>
> • A leader must demonstrate capability to lead.
>
> • A leader must have an evident call from God.
>
> ii. The elders of Israel received David's leadership when they saw these things in David. When we see these same things in leaders, we should also receive their leadership.

e. **And they anointed David king over Israel**: 1 Chronicles 12:23-40 describes the great assembly that gathered in Hebron to recognize David as king over all Israel. Chronicles describes the impressive army that came to Hebron and numbers the soldiers at over 340,000 men. It then describes the scene: *All these men of war, who could keep ranks, came to Hebron with a loyal heart, to make David king over all Israel; and all the rest of Israel were of one mind to make David king. And they were there with David three days, eating and drinking, for their brethren had prepared for them... for there was joy in Israel.* (1 Chronicles 12:38-40)

2. (4-5) The duration of David's reign.

David *was* thirty years old when he began to reign, *and* he reigned forty years. In Hebron he reigned over Judah seven years and six months, and in Jerusalem he reigned thirty-three years over all Israel and Judah.

a. **David was thirty years old**: This is a good measuring point for David's life. Samuel anointed David when he was about 15, and he did not take the throne until 30. David spent at least 15 years in preparation for the throne of Israel.

b. **In Hebron he reigned... in Jerusalem he reigned**: All told, David reigned 40 years. His 15 years of preparation were not too long compared to his reign. God uses great preparation when the task is great.

B. David captures Jerusalem.

1. (6-8) The capture of Jerusalem.

And the king and his men went to Jerusalem against the Jebusites, the inhabitants of the land, who spoke to David, saying, "You shall not come in here; but the blind and the lame will repel you," thinking, "David cannot come in here." Nevertheless David took the stronghold of Zion

(that *is,* the City of David). Now David said on that day, "Whoever climbs up by way of the water shaft and defeats the Jebusites (the lame and the blind, *who are* hated by David's soul), *he shall be chief and captain.*" Therefore they say, "The blind and the lame shall not come into the house."

a. **The king and his men went to Jerusalem against the Jebusites**: Up to this time Jerusalem was a small Canaanite city in the center of Israel. Some 400 years after God commanded Israel to take the whole land, this city was still in Canaanite hands.

b. **You shall not come in here; but the blind and the lame will repel you**: Because of its location, Jerusalem was an easily defended city. This made the Jebusites overconfident and quick to mock David and his troops.

c. **Nevertheless David took the stronghold of Zion**: Despite the difficulty, David and his men took the city. Since the **water shaft** is mentioned, some think that David sent his men through what is called "Warren's Shaft." Whatever exactly their tactics, David and his men persisted through difficult circumstances to defeat an overconfident enemy.

i. On the same principle, King Jesus conquers old strongholds when he becomes king over our lives. Territory that should have been given to Him long ago is now conquered. "I want to say to you in the name of the Lord Jesus that there is no habit that has gone so deep but that the power of the blood of Jesus can go deeper, and there is no entrenchment of sin that has gone so far but the power of the risen Lord, by His Holy Spirit, can go further." (Redpath)

2. (9-10) Jerusalem is David's new capital city.

Then David dwelt in the stronghold, and called it the City of David. And David built all around from the Millo and inward. So David went on and became great, and the LORD God of hosts *was* with him.

a. **David dwelt in the stronghold**: Jerusalem became the capital city of David's kingdom. It was a good choice because:

- It had no prior tribal association and was therefore good for a unified Israel.

- The geography of the city made it easy to defend against a hostile army.

b. **So David went on and became great**: David knew greatness, but he was by no means an "overnight success." David was long prepared for the greatness he later enjoyed, and he came to the place of greatness because **the LORD God of hosts was with him.**

i. In God's plan there is almost always a hidden price of greatness. Often those who become great among God's people experience much pain and difficulty in God's training process.

3. (11-12) David's palace and greatness.

Then Hiram king of Tyre sent messengers to David, and cedar trees, and carpenters and masons. And they built David a house. So David knew that the LORD had established him as king over Israel, and that He had exalted His kingdom for the sake of His people Israel.

a. **They built David a house**: This showed David's influence and importance. Neighboring kings honored him with the finest craftsmen and wood to build a palace. This relationship with **Hiram king of Tyre** also showed that David was more than a man of war. He knew how to build important political alliances.

b. **So David knew**: David knew three things that made his reign great. Every godly leader should know these three things well.

- **David knew that the LORD had established him as king over Israel**: David knew that God called him and established him over Israel.

- **He had exalted His kingdom**: David knew that the kingdom belonged to God - it was **His kingdom**.

- **For the sake of His people Israel**: David knew God wanted to use him as a channel to bless His people. It was not for David's sake that he was lifted up, but for the **sake of His people Israel**.

4. (13-16) David's many wives.

And David took more concubines and wives from Jerusalem, after he had come from Hebron. Also more sons and daughters were born to David. Now these *are* the names of those who were born to him in Jerusalem: Shammua, Shobab, Nathan, Solomon, Ibhar, Elishua, Nepheg, Japhia, Elishama, Eliada, and Eliphelet.

a. **David took more concubines and wives**: This was in direct disobedience to Deuteronomy 17:17: *Neither shall he multiply wives for himself, lest his heart turn away.*

b. **More sons and daughters were born to David**: Certainly David (and everyone else) saw these many children as God's sign of blessing upon David and his many marriages. Yet most of the trouble to come in David's life came from his relationships with women and problems with his children.

i. It is often true that the seeds to our future trouble are sown in times of great success and prosperity. In some ways, David handled trials better than success.

C. David defeats the Philistines.

1. (17-19) David fights against Israel's old enemies.

Now when the Philistines heard that they had anointed David king over Israel, all the Philistines went up to search for David. And David heard *of it* **and went down to the stronghold. The Philistines also went and deployed themselves in the Valley of Rephaim. So David inquired of the LORD, saying, "Shall I go up against the Philistines? Will You deliver them into my hand?" And the LORD said to David, "Go up, for I will doubtless deliver the Philistines into your hand."**

a. **The Philistines also went and deployed themselves**: David's success brought new challenges from the *outside*. As God worked mightily in David's life, the devil also got to work and brought opposition against David.

b. **David inquired of the LORD**: As David sought God and looked to Him for guidance, he was blessed. God honored David's dependence on Him and gave him the promise of victory.

2. (20-21) David defeats the Philistines at Baal Perazim.

So David went to Baal Perazim, and David defeated them there; and he said, "The LORD has broken through my enemies before me, like a breakthrough of water." Therefore he called the name of that place Baal Perazim. And they left their images there, and David and his men carried them away.

a. **The LORD has broken through my enemies before me**: At the battle of **Baal Perazim**, David defeated the Philistines with an overwhelming force, **like a breakthrough of water**.

b. **They left their images there, and David and his men carried them away**: The Philistines brought their idols to the battle, thinking they would help defeat the Israelites. Because David inquired of God and obeyed God, they carried away the Philistine idols.

3. (22-25) David defeats the Philistines at the Valley of Rephaim.

Then the Philistines went up once again and deployed themselves in the Valley of Rephaim. Therefore David inquired of the LORD, and He said, "You shall not go up; circle around behind them, and come upon them in front of the mulberry trees. And it shall be, when you hear the sound of marching in the tops of the mulberry trees, then you shall advance

quickly. For then the LORD will go out before you to strike the camp of the Philistines." And David did so, as the LORD commanded him; and he drove back the Philistines from Geba as far as Gezer.

a. **David inquired of the LORD**: After the first victory over the Philistines, David was wise enough to wait on the LORD before the second battle. It is easy for many in the same situation to say, "I've fought this battle before. I know how to win. This will be easy." *David always triumphed when he sought and obeyed God.*

b. **You shall not go up; circle around them**: God directed David differently in this battle. Even against the same enemy, not every battle is the same.

> i. In his commentary on this passage, Adam Clarke noted the remarkable guidance of God in David's life and asked a good question. "How is it that such supernatural directions and assistances are not communicated now? Because they are not asked for; and they are not asked for because they are not expected; and they are not expected because men have not faith; and they have not faith because they are under a refined spirit of atheism, and have no spiritual intercourse with their Maker." (Clarke)

c. **The LORD will go out before you to strike the camp of the Philistines**: At the battle of **Rephaim** David waited for the LORD to **strike the camp** of the enemy first. The sign of the LORD's work was **the sound of marching in the tops of the mulberry trees**.

> i. "As the Rabbis have it, and it is a very pretty conceit if it be true, the footsteps of angels walking along the tops of the mulberry trees make them rustle; that was the sign for them to fight, when God's cherubim were going with them, when they should come, who can walk through the clouds and fly through the air, led by the great Captain himself, walking along the mulberry trees, and so make a rustle by their celestial footsteps." (Spurgeon)

> ii. At the signal that the LORD was at work, David and his troops rushed forward to victory. This principle is true in our every-day walk with God. When we sense that the Lord is at work, we must **advance quickly**, and we will see a great victory won. "We must also, in the spiritual warfare, observe and obey the motions of the Spirit, when he setteth up his standard; for those are the sounds of God's goings, the footsteps of his anointed." (Trapp)

> iii. There is something wonderful about the King James Version translation of 2 Samuel 5:24: *when thou hearest the sound of a going in the tops of the mulberry trees, that then thou shalt bestir thyself.* When

you hear the work of God happening, *bestir thyself* - **advance quickly**. Spurgeon liked to point out that it said *bestir thyself* - often we think we must stir others up. That often just becomes hype and emotionalism. Instead, stir yourself.

iv. When we see the work of God happening around us, it is like the sound in the mulberry trees - the rustling sound should awaken us to prayer and devotion. A time of crisis or tragedy is also like the sound in the mulberry trees - the rustling sound should awaken us to confession and repentance. "Now, what should I do? The first thing I will do is, I will bestir myself. But how shall I do it? Why, I will go home this day, and I will wrestle in prayer more earnestly than I have been wont to do that God will bless the minister, and multiply the church." (Spurgeon)

2 Samuel 6 - David Brings the Ark of God into Jerusalem

Psalm 132 is commonly associated with the events of this chapter.

A. The failed first attempt.

1. (1-2) Bringing the ark of God to Jerusalem.

Again David gathered all *the* choice *men* of Israel, thirty thousand. And David arose and went with all the people who *were* with him from Baale Judah to bring up from there the ark of God, whose name is called by the Name, the LORD of Hosts, who dwells *between* the cherubim.

a. **David gathered all the choice men of Israel**: David gathered so many of his best soldiers because bringing the ark to Jerusalem was an important step towards providing a central place of worship for all of Israel.

b. **To bring up from there the ark of God**: This was the *Ark of the Covenant*, which God commanded Moses to make more than 400 years before David's time. It was a wood box (the word **ark** means "box" or "chest") completely covered with gold and with an ornate gold lid or top known as the *mercy seat*.

i. The **ark of God** was 3 feet 9 inches (1.15 meters) long, 2 feet 3 inches (.68 meter) wide and 2 feet 3 inches (.68 meter) high. In it were the tablets of the law that Moses brought down from Mount Sinai, a jar of manna, and Aaron's rod that miraculously budded as a confirmation of his leadership.

c. **The LORD of Hosts, who dwells between the cherubim**: The **ark of God** represented the immediate presence and glory of God in Israel. David considered it a high priority to bring the ark out of obscurity and back into prominence. David wanted Israel to be alive with a sense of the near presence and glory of God.

i. The last mention of the **ark of God** was when it came back from the land of the Philistines in 1 Samuel 7:1. It sat at the house of Abinadab for some 70 years. David had a great motive - to emphasize the presence and glory of God in Israel.

2. (3-5) The Ark is brought out with great joy.

So they set the ark of God on a new cart, and brought it out of the house of Abinadab, which *was* on the hill; and Uzzah and Ahio, the sons of Abinadab, drove the new cart. And they brought it out of the house of Abinadab, which *was* on the hill, accompanying the ark of God; and Ahio went before the ark. Then David and all the house of Israel played *music* before the Lord on all kinds of *instruments of* fir wood, on harps, on stringed instruments, on tambourines, on sistrums, and on cymbals.

a. **So they set the ark of God on a new cart**: Transporting the ark on a cart was against God's specific command. The ark was designed to be carried (Exodus 25:12-15) and was only to be carried by Levites of the family of Koath (Numbers 4:15).

i. God wanted the ark to be carried because He wanted nothing mechanical about the ark, representing His presence. "The ark was nothing less than the burden of the Lord, and the burden of the Lord was to be carried on the hearts of the Levites." (Redpath)

ii. We can imagine what these men thought. "Look - we have a **new cart** for the ark of God. God will be very pleased at our fancy **new cart**." They thought that a new technology or luxury could cover over their ignorant disobedience.

iii. "We want God's presence very much, don't we? But we like to hitch His presence to some of our new carts. We like to add Him to our list of organizations, to load Him on top of the mechanics of a busy life, and then drive. How much of our service is really in the energy of the flesh, I wonder! So often we put forth our hands, but not our hearts." (Redpath)

iv. "It is not new things we need, but *new fire*." (John Wesley)

v. The Philistines transported the ark on a cart in 1 Samuel 6:10-11. They got away with it because they were Philistines, but God expected more from His people. Israel was to take their example from God's Word, not from the innovations of the Philistines.

b. **Uzzah and Ahio, the sons of Abinadab, drove the new cart**: The meaning of the names of these sons of Abinadab paint a meaningful picture. **Uzzah** means "strength" and **Ahio** means "friendly."

i. Much service for the Lord is like this - a new cart, a big production, with *strength* leading and *friendly* out front - yet all done without inquiring of God or looking to His will. Surely David prayed for God's blessing on this big production, but he didn't inquire of God regarding the production itself. This was a good thing done the wrong way.

c. **Then David and all the house of Israel played music before the LORD**: Judging from the importance of the occasion and all the instruments mentioned, this was quite a production. The atmosphere was joyful, exciting, and engaging. The problem was that none of it pleased God because it was all in disobedience to His word.

i. We are often tempted to judge a worship experience by how it makes *us* feel. But when we realize that worship is about *pleasing God*, we are driven to His word, so we can know how He wants to be worshipped.

ii. It is hard to receive it in our consumer-oriented culture, but worship *isn't all about what pleases us*. It's all about what pleases God.

3. (6-7) Uzzah is struck dead for touching the ark.

And when they came to Nachon's threshing floor, Uzzah put out *his hand* to the ark of God and took hold of it, for the oxen stumbled. Then the anger of the LORD was aroused against Uzzah, and God struck him there for *his* error; and he died there by the ark of God.

a. **When they came to Nachon's threshing floor**: At a **threshing floor** the whole stalks of wheat were gathered, and the *chaff* was separated from the *wheat*. There was a lot of *chaff* in this production, and God blew away the chaff at **Nachon's threshing floor**.

b. **Uzzah put out his hand to the ark of God and took hold of it**: This was strictly forbidden. Regarding the transporting of the ark Numbers 4:15 says, *they shall not touch any holy thing lest they die.*

i. Uzzah made a decision in a moment to disregard God's command and to do what seemed right to him. Even decisions made in a moment matter before God.

c. **God struck him there for his error**: God fulfilled the ominous promise of Numbers 4:15 and **struck** Uzzah. David wanted Israel to know the presence of the LORD and God showed up at **Nachon's threshing floor** - but not in the way anyone wanted.

i. Uzzah's **error** was more than just a reflex action or instinct. God **struck** Uzzah because his action was based upon a critical **error** in thinking.

- Uzzah erred in thinking it didn't matter who carried the ark.
- Uzzah erred in thinking it didn't matter how the ark was carried.

- Uzzah erred in thinking he knew all about the ark because it was in his father's house for so long.

- Uzzah erred in thinking that God couldn't take care of the ark of Himself.

- Uzzah erred in thinking that the ground of Nachon's threshing floor was less holy than his own hand.

ii. "He saw no difference between the ark and any other valuable article. His intention to help was right enough; but there was a profound insensibility to the awful sacredness of the ark, on which even its Levitical bearers were forbidden to lay hands." (Maclaren)

4. (8-9) David reacts with anger and fear.

And David became angry because of the LORD's outbreak against Uzzah; and he called the name of the place Perez Uzzah to this day. David was afraid of the LORD that day; and he said, "How can the ark of the LORD come to me?"

a. **David became angry because of the LORD's outbreak**: David's anger was based in confusion. He couldn't understand why his good intentions weren't enough. God cares about both our intentions and actions.

b. **How can the ark of the LORD come to me**: David knew it was important to bring the **ark of the LORD** into the center of Israel's life. He wanted all Israel to be excited about the presence and glory of God. Because of what happened to Uzzah, David felt he couldn't do what God wanted him to do.

i. David's response in the rest of the chapter shows that he found the answer to his question. He answered the question with the thought later expressed in Isaiah 8:20: *To the law and to the testimony!* David found the answer in God's word.

B. The successful second attempt.

1. (10-12a) David leaves the ark with Obed-Edom.

So David would not move the ark of the LORD with him into the City of David; but David took it aside into the house of Obed-Edom the Gittite. The ark of the LORD remained in the house of Obed-Edom the Gittite three months. And the LORD blessed Obed-Edom and all his household. Now it was told King David, saying, "The LORD has blessed the house of Obed-Edom and all that *belongs* to him, because of the ark of God."

a. **David took it aside into the house of Obed-Edom**: David did this in fulfillment of God's word. **Obed-Edom** was a Levite of the family of Koath (1 Chronicles 26:4). This was the family within the tribe of Levi that God commanded to carry and take care of the ark (Numbers 4:15).

b. **And the Lord blessed Obed-Edom and all his household**: When God's Word was obeyed, and His holiness was respected blessing followed. God wanted the ark to be a blessing for Israel, not a curse. We might say that the curse didn't come from God's heart but from man's disobedience.

2. (12b-15) The ark successfully comes to Jerusalem.

So David went and brought up the ark of God from the house of Obed-Edom to the City of David with gladness. And so it was, when those bearing the ark of the Lord had gone six paces, that he sacrificed oxen and fatted sheep. Then David danced before the Lord with all *his* might; and David *was* wearing a linen ephod. So David and all the house of Israel brought up the ark of the Lord with shouting and with the sound of the trumpet.

a. **So David went and brought up the ark of God from the house of Obed-Edom to the City of David with gladness**: David was glad to know that the presence and glory of God could bring blessing instead of a curse. He was also glad to see that when they obeyed God they were blessed.

i. David explained to the priests why God struck out against them in their first attempt to bring the ark to Jerusalem in 1 Chronicles 15:13: *For because you did not do it the first time, the Lord our God broke out against us, because we did not consult Him about the proper order.*

ii. When the worship was in *the proper order* it was still filled **with gladness** and joy. It is a mistake to feel that "real" worship must be subdued, solemn, or only in a minor key.

b. **When those bearing the ark of the Lord had gone six paces, that he sacrificed oxen and fatted sheep**: This was elaborate, excessive, over-the-top sacrifice. This excess of sacrifice communicated *atonement, consecration,* and *longing for fellowship.*

i. 1 Chronicles 15:11-15 shows us that David specifically commanded the priests to carry the ark the right way - on their shoulders. We often think that a "new cart" or "strength" or a "friendly" manner is the way to bring the presence and glory of God. But God always wants His presence and glory to come on the shoulders of consecrated, obedient, praising men and women.

ii. It also showed that David brought the ark to Jerusalem with a big production - bigger than the first attempt. David was wise enough to know that the problem with the first attempt wasn't that it was a big production, but that it was a big production that came from man and not God.

c. **David danced before the LORD with all his might**: David didn't hold back anything in his own expression of worship. He didn't dance out of obligation but out of heartfelt worship. He was glad to bring the **ark of the LORD** into Jerusalem according to God's word.

> i. This expression of David's heart showed that he had a genuine *emotional link* to God. There are two great errors in this area - the error of making emotions the center of our Christian life and the error of an emotionally detached Christian life. In the Christian life, emotions must not be manipulated, and they must not be repressed.

> ii. We don't think that dancing is strange when the baseball player rounds the bases after the game winning home run. We don't think it is strange when the winning touchdown is scored or when our own child scores a goal. We think nothing at hands raised at a concert or a touchdown. We should not think them strange in worship to God.

d. **David was wearing a linen ephod**: It is a mistake to think that David was immodest. 1 Chronicles 15:27 indicates that David was dressed just like all the other priests and Levites in this procession.

> i. From our knowledge of ancient and modern culture, we can surmise that David's dance wasn't a solo performance. He probably danced with simple rhythmic steps together with other men in the way one might see Orthodox Jewish men today dance. In this context, David's **linen ephod** means he set aside his royal robes and dressed just like everyone else in the procession.

> ii. We might also point out that David's dancing was appropriate in the context. This was a parade with a marching band, a grand procession. David's dancing fit right in. If David did this as the nation gathered on the Day of Atonement, it would be out of context and wrong.

3. (16-19) David brings everyone present into the worship experience and the fellowship meal.

Now as the ark of the LORD came into the City of David, Michal, Saul's daughter, looked through a window and saw King David leaping and whirling before the LORD; and she despised him in her heart. So they brought the ark of the LORD, and set it in its place in the midst of the tabernacle that David had erected for it. Then David offered burnt offerings and peace offerings before the LORD. And when David had finished offering burnt offerings and peace offerings, he blessed the people in the name of the LORD of hosts. Then he distributed among all the people, among the whole multitude of Israel, both the women

and the men, to everyone a loaf of bread, a piece *of meat,* and a cake of raisins. So all the people departed, everyone to his house.

> a. **She despised him in her heart**: David's wife Michal didn't appreciate David's exuberant worship. She felt it wasn't dignified for the King of Israel to express his emotions before God.

>> i. "No doubt, there are particularly nice and dainty people who will censure God's chosen if they live wholly to his praise, and they will call them eccentric, old-fashioned, obstinate, absurd, and I don't know what besides. From the window of their superiority they look down upon us." (Spurgeon)

> b. **They brought the ark of the LORD, and set it in its place in the midst of the tabernacle**: After many years - since the ark was lost in battle - the ark was returned to the **tabernacle** and set in the most holy place. The emblem of God's presence and glory was set at its proper place in Israel.

> c. **Then David offered burnt offerings and peace offerings before the LORD**: The **burnt offerings** spoke of *consecration.* The **peace offerings** spoke of *fellowship.* This was a day of great consecration and fellowship with God. It was also a great barbeque.

4. (20) Michal's complaint.

Then David returned to bless his household. And Michal the daughter of Saul came out to meet David, and said, "How glorious was the king of Israel today, uncovering himself today in the eyes of the maids of his servants, as one of the base fellows shamelessly uncovers himself!"

> a. **David returned to bless his household**: After this day of great victory David came home to bring a blessing to his whole family.

> b. **How glorious was the king of Israel today**: With biting sarcasm, Michal's criticism could have ruined this whole day for David. He might have expected such an attack after such a remarkable day of victory. "Pirates look out for loaded vessels." (Spurgeon)

> c. **Uncovering himself today**: Michal seemed to indicate that she didn't object to David's dancing, but to what David wore when he set aside his royal robes and danced as a man just like the other men celebrating in the procession. David acted as if he were just another worshipper in Israel.

5. (21-23) David's rebuke of Michal.

So David said to Michal, *"It was* before the LORD, who chose me instead of your father and all his house, to appoint me ruler over the people of the LORD, over Israel. Therefore I will play *music* before the LORD. And I will be even more undignified than this, and will be humble in my own

sight. But as for the maidservants of whom you have spoken, by them I will be held in honor." Therefore Michal the daughter of Saul had no children to the day of her death.

a. **It was before the LORD**: David didn't let Michal's sarcastic criticism ruin his day. He simply explained the truth: "I did it for God, not for you."

i. This is not a justification for everything in the context of worship. When David considered the context of the procession and the whole setting, his conscience was clear. He knew his dancing wasn't inappropriate to the setting or context. Someone who acts inappropriately to the setting or context of a meeting can't simply justify it by saying, "**It was before the LORD**."

b. **To appoint me ruler over the people of the LORD**: "David did not say, 'Over my people': he acknowledged that they were not his people, but Jehovah's people. He was only lieutenant-governor; the Lord was still the great King of Israel." (Spurgeon)

c. **And will be humble in my own sight**: What David did was *humbling* to him. He didn't dance to show others how spiritual he was.

i. "David would more and more abase himself before the Lord. He felt that whatever Michal's opinion of him might be, it could not be more humbling than his own view of himself. Brother, if any man thinks ill of you, do not be angry with him; for you are worse than he thinks you to be." (Spurgeon)

d. **Therefore Michal the daughter of Saul had no children to the day of her death**: Michal's barrenness was not necessarily the result of Divine judgment. It may be that David never had marital relations with her again. Nevertheless, the principle stands: there is often barrenness in the life and ministry of the overly critical.

2 Samuel 7 - God's Covenant with David

A. David proposes to build God a permanent house.

1. (1-3) Nathan's premature advice to David.

Now it came to pass when the king was dwelling in his house, and the LORD had given him rest from all his enemies all around, that the king said to Nathan the prophet, "See now, I dwell in a house of cedar, but the ark of God dwells inside tent curtains." Then Nathan said to the king, "Go, do all that *is* in your heart, for the LORD *is* with you."

a. **The LORD had given him rest from all his enemies all around**: This leads us to believe that the events of 2 Samuel 7 happened after the wars of conquest described in 2 Samuel 8. This section is placed before the war accounts in the text to show its greater importance.

b. **I dwell in a house of cedar**: **Cedar** wood was especially valued. This meant that David lived in an expensive, beautiful home. When he remembered that **the ark of God dwells inside tent curtains**, the contrast bothered him. David was troubled by the thought that he lived in a nicer house than the ark of the covenant.

    i. **A house of cedar**: "It was a remarkable contrast to the shelter of Adullam's cave." (Meyer)

    ii. Without saying the specific words, David told Nathan that he wanted to build a *temple* to replace the *tabernacle*. When Israel was in the wilderness more than 400 years before this, God commanded Moses to build a tent of meeting according to a specific pattern (Exodus 25:8-9). God never asked for a permanent building to replace the tent, but now David wanted to do this for God.

    iii. The tent of meeting - also known as the tabernacle - was perfectly suited to Israel in the wilderness because they constantly moved. Now that Israel was securely in the land and the ark of the covenant was in Jerusalem (2 Samuel 6:17), David thought it would be better and more appropriate to build a temple to replace the tabernacle.

c. **Go, do all that is in your heart, for the LORD is with you**: Nathan said this to David because it seemed good and reasonable. What could be wrong with David building a temple?

i. **All that is in your heart** shows that David's heart was filled with this question: "What can I do for God?" He was so filled with gratitude and concern for God's glory that he wanted to do something special for God.

2. (4-7) God's response to David's offer.

But it happened that night that the word of the LORD came to Nathan, saying, "Go and tell My servant David, 'Thus says the LORD: "Would you build a house for Me to dwell in? For I have not dwelt in a house since the time that I brought the children of Israel up from Egypt, even to this day, but have moved about in a tent and in a tabernacle. Wherever I have moved about with all the children of Israel, have I ever spoken a word to anyone from the tribes of Israel, whom I commanded to shepherd My people Israel, saying, 'Why have you not built Me a house of cedar?'"

a. **That night that the word of the LORD came to Nathan**: Nathan's response to David was presumptuous. He answered according to human judgment and common sense, but before he heard the **word of the LORD**.

i. "It is of the utmost importance that we should ever test our desires, even the highest and holiest of them, by His will. Work, excellent in itself, should never be undertaken, save at the express command of God. The passing of time will always vindicate the wisdom of the Divine will." (Morgan)

b. **Would you build a house for Me to dwell in**: God seemed honored and "surprised" that David offered to build Him a house. It was as if God said to David, "You want to build Me a house? No one ever offered to do that before, and I never commanded anyone to do it."

i. David wanted to do more than God commanded. This is a wonderful place to be in our relationship with God. Most of us are so stuck in the thinking, "How little can I do and still please the LORD?" that we never really want to do *more* than God commands.

ii. "Though the Lord refused to David the realization of his wish, he did it in a most gracious manner. He did not put the idea away from him in anger or disdain, as though David had cherished an unworthy desire; but he honored his servant even in the non-acceptance of his offer." (Spurgeon)

c. **Would you build a house**: David now learned that God didn't want him to build the temple, but David didn't respond by doing *nothing*. According to 1 Chronicles 29:2-9, David gathered all the materials for building the temple so that Solomon could build a glorious house for God.

i. "If you cannot have what you hoped, do not sit down in despair and allow the energies of your life to run to waste; but arise, and gird yourself to help others to achieve. If you may not build, you may gather materials for him that shall. If you may not go down the mine, you can hold the ropes." (Meyer)

B. God proposes to build David a permanent house.

1. (8-9) God reminds David what He has done for him.

"Now therefore, thus shall you say to My servant David, 'Thus says the LORD of hosts: "I took you from the sheepfold, from following the sheep, to be ruler over My people, over Israel. And I have been with you wherever you have gone, and have cut off all your enemies from before you, and have made you a great name, like the name of the great men who *are* on the earth."'"

a. **I took you from the sheepfold, from following the sheep, to be ruler over My people**: God took David from the pasture to the throne.

b. **I have been with you wherever you have gone**: God protected David from all his enemies.

c. **Have made you a great name**: God made David's name great in all the earth.

2. (10-11) God promises two things to David.

"Moreover I will appoint a place for My people Israel, and will plant them, that they may dwell in a place of their own and move no more; nor shall the sons of wickedness oppress them anymore, as previously, since the time that I commanded judges *to be* over My people Israel, and have caused you to rest from all your enemies. Also the LORD tells you that He will make you a house."

a. **I will appoint a place for My people Israel**: God promised David that under his reign, He would establish a permanent and secure Israel. God promised this first because He knew that David, being a godly shepherd, was first concerned about the welfare of his people.

b. **He will make you a house**: God promised David that He would build *him* a house in the sense of establishing a dynasty for the house of David. This was an enduring legacy for David long after his death.

i. David wanted to build God a temple. God said, "Thank you David, but no thanks. Let Me build you a **house** instead." This was a greater promise than David's offer to God, because David's "house" (dynasty) would last longer and be more glorious than the temple David wanted to build.

ii. God honored what David gave Him, even though he only gave it to God in his sincere intention. There are some things that we *want* to give God but are prevented from giving. In these cases, God receives the *intention* as the *gift*.

iii. God said "No" to David's offer because David was a man of war, and God wanted a man of peace to build His temple. 1 Chronicles 22:8-10 explains this: *But the word of the LORD came to me, saying, 'You have shed much blood and have made great wars; you shall not build a house for My name, because you have shed much blood on the earth in My sight... a son shall be born to you, who shall be a man of rest... He shall be build a house for My name.*

iv. The explanation to David recorded in 1 Chronicles 22:8 came years afterwards. We can surmise that for many years David did not know the exact reason why God didn't want him to build the temple. "It would have wounded David needlessly to have been told this at the time... Meanwhile David possessed his soul in patience, and said to himself, 'God has a reason; I cannot understand it, but it is well.'" (Meyer)

3. (12-17) God details His promise of a house for David.

"When your days are fulfilled and you rest with your fathers, I will set up your seed after you, who will come from your body, and I will establish his kingdom. He shall build a house for My name, and I will establish the throne of his kingdom forever. I will be his Father, and he shall be My son. If he commits iniquity, I will chasten him with the rod of men and with the blows of the sons of men. But My mercy shall not depart from him, as I took *it* from Saul, whom I removed from before you. And your house and your kingdom shall be established forever before you. Your throne shall be established forever." According to all these words and according to all this vision, so Nathan spoke to David.

a. **I will set up your seed after you**: In this, God specifically promised a hereditary monarchy for the house of David. It was important for God to repeat this promise specifically because there had never yet been a king succeeded by his son in Israel.

i. "The family of Saul became *totally extinct*; the family of David remained till the incarnation." (Clarke)

ii. This great promise that God made to David had only a *future* fulfillment. David would only benefit *in his day* from the promise through faith. If David had a "what's-in-it-for-me-right-now" attitude, the promise would mean nothing to him.

iii. "The joy which filled David's bosom was a spiritual one, because he knew that Jesus would come of his race, and that an everlasting kingdom would be set up in his person, and in him should the Gentiles trust." (Spurgeon)

b. **He shall build a house for My name**: Though David would not build a temple for God, David's descendent would.

c. **I will establish the throne of his kingdom forever**: The family of David did rule over Israel for more than four centuries but was eventually removed because of evil added upon evil. Yet out of the "stump" of Jesse, God raised up a new branch that will reign for ever and ever (Isaiah 11:1-2).

d. **I will be his Father, and he shall be My son. If he commits iniquity, I will chasten him**: This descendent of David will enjoy a special relationship with God. If he sins, God will not reject him. Instead, God will **chasten** him without rejecting him.

e. **Your throne shall be established forever**: God promisesd David that the reign of his dynasty would last forever.

i. Each of these great promises was *partially* fulfilled in Solomon, David's son and successor to his throne.

- Solomon ruled on David's throne.

- God's mercies never departed from Solomon, though he sinned.

- Solomon built God a magnificent house.

ii. But the prophets foretold a greater fulfillment of these promises.

- *Behold, the days are coming, says the Lord, that I will raise to David a Branch of righteousness; a King shall reign and prosper, and execute righteousness in the earth. . . Now this is His name by which He will be called: THE LORD OUR RIGHTEOUSNESS.* (Jeremiah 23:5-6)

- *For unto us a Child is born, unto us a Son is given; and the government will be upon His shoulder. . . Upon the throne of David and over His kingdom, to order it and establish it... from that time forward, even forever.* (Isaiah 9:6-7)

- *And behold, you will conceive in your womb and bring forth a Son, and shall call His name JESUS. He will be great, and will be called the Son of the Highest; and the Lord God will give Him the throne of His father David. And He will reign over the house of Jacob forever, and of His kingdom there will be no end.* (Luke 1:31-33)

iii. God's promise of a house for David is completely fulfilled in Jesus Christ.

- Jesus does reign and will reign on David's throne forever.

- The Father's mercies never departed from Jesus, even when He was made sin for us.

- Jesus is building the Father a magnificent house (Hebrews 3:3-6) in the sense that we are God's temple (1 Peter 2:5) and the church is God's new house.

C. David's prayer of thanksgiving.

1. (18-24) He humbly glorifies God for His goodness.

Then King David went in and sat before the LORD; and he said: "Who *am* I, O Lord GOD? And what is my house, that You have brought me this far? And yet this was a small thing in Your sight, O Lord GOD; and You have also spoken of Your servant's house for a great while to come. *Is* this the manner of man, O Lord GOD? Now what more can David say to You? For You, Lord GOD, know Your servant. For Your word's sake, and according to Your own heart, You have done all these great things, to make Your servant know *them.* Therefore You are great, O Lord GOD. For *there is* none like You, nor *is there any* God besides You, according to all that we have heard with our ears. And who *is* like Your people, like Israel, the one nation on the earth whom God went to redeem for Himself as a people, to make for Himself a name—and to do for Youself great and awesome deeds for Your land—before Your people whom You redeemed for Yourself from Egypt, the nations, and their gods? For You have made Your people Israel Your very own people forever; and You, LORD, have become their God."

a. **Who am I, O Lord GOD?... Therefore You are great, O Lord GOD:** When David received this spectacular gift, he didn't think it made *him* any greater. In David's eyes it made *God* greater.

i. David's attitude wasn't, "I am so great that even God's gives me gifts." His attitude was, "God is so great that He gives even me gifts."

We should receive salvation and every blessing with the same attitude. God's giving reflects the greatness of the Giver, not the receiver.

b. **Your servant**: David's humble reception of this gift is shown by the repetition of the phrase **Your servant** - ten times in this prayer.

i. It shows that David humbly accepted God's "no" when he wanted to build the temple. "There are some professors who would do a great thing if they might, but if they are not permitted to act a shining part they are in the sulks and angry with their God. David when his proposal was set aside found it in his heart not to murmur, but to pray." (Spurgeon)

2. (25-29) David boldly asks that the promise be fulfilled as spoken.

"Now, O LORD God, the word which You have spoken concerning Your servant and concerning his house, establish *it* forever and do as You have said. So let Your name be magnified forever, saying, 'The LORD of hosts *is* the God over Israel.' And let the house of Your servant David be established before You. For You, O LORD of hosts, God of Israel, have revealed *this* to Your servant, saying, 'I will build you a house.' Therefore Your servant has found it in his heart to pray this prayer to You. And now, O Lord GOD, You are God, and Your words are true, and You have promised this goodness to Your servant. Now therefore, let it please You to bless the house of Your servant, that it may continue forever before You; for You, O Lord GOD, have spoken *it*, and with Your blessing let the house of Your servant be blessed forever."

a. **Establish it forever and do as You have said**: David's prayer boldly asked God to *do* what He *promised*. This wasn't *passive* prayer that said, "Well God, do whatever You want to do - I don't really care one way or another." This wasn't *arrogant* prayer that said, "Well God, let me tell You what to do." This was *bold* prayer that said, "God, here is Your promise - now I trust You to fulfill it grandly and to be faithful to Your word."

i. The phrase "**therefore Your servant has found it in his heart to pray this prayer to You**" emphasizes this. David said, "I'm only praying because You promised. You told me that this is what You want to do."

ii. "God sent the promise on purpose to be used. If I see a Bank of England note, it is a promise for a certain amount of money, and I take it and use it. But oh I my friend, do try and use God's promises; nothing pleases God better than to see his promises put in circulation; he loves to see his children bring them up to him, and say, 'Lord, do as thou hast said.' And let me tell you that it glorifies God to use his promises." (Spurgeon)

iii. This kind of prayer *appropriates* God's promise. Just because God promised doesn't mean that we possess. Through believing prayer like this, God promises, and we appropriate. If we don't appropriate in faith, God's promise is left unclaimed.

- We may appropriate His promise for forgiveness: *If we confess our sins, He is faithful and just to forgive us our sins and to cleanse us from all unrighteousness.* (1 John 1:9)

- We may appropriate His promise for peace: *Peace I leave with you, My peace I give to you: not as the world gives do I give to you. Let not your heart be troubled, neither let it be afraid.* (John 14:27)

- We may appropriate His promise for guidance: *I will instruct you and teach you in the way you should go: I will guide you with My eye.* (Psalm 32:8)

- We may appropriate His promise for growth: *He who has begun a good work in you will complete it until the day of Jesus Christ.* (Philippians 1:6)

- We may appropriate His promise for help: *Let us therefore come boldly to the throne of grace, that we may obtain mercy and find grace of help in time of need.* (Hebrews 4:16)

b. **Therefore Your servant has found it in his heart to pray this prayer to You**: Notice that David prayed from the **heart**. Some people pray from a book; others pray from their head. The right place to pray from is the **heart**.

i. It also says that David came before God to **pray this prayer**. Some prayers are not *prayed*. They are said or read or thought, but not *prayed*. "Not to say this prayer, but to pray this prayer. There is great force in the expression. Some prayers are never prayed, but are like arrows which are never shot from the bow. Scarcely may I call them prayers, for they are such as to form, and matter, and verbiage, but they are said, not prayed. The praying of prayer is the main matter." (Spurgeon)

c. **You are God, and Your words are true**: This was David's foundation of faith. He knew that God was **God**, and that every word of His was **true**. He knew that God can be trusted.

i. "The great sin of not believing in the Lord Jesus Christ is often spoken of very lightly and in a very trifling spirit, as though it were scarcely any sin at all; yet, according to my text, and, indeed, according to the whole tenor of the Scriptures, unbelief is the giving of God the lie, and what can be worse?" (Spurgeon)

2 Samuel 8 - The Wars of David

A. David's many wars.

1. (1) David subdues the Philistines.

After this it came to pass that David attacked the Philistines and subdued them. And David took Metheg Ammah from the hand of the Philistines.

a. **David attacked the Philistines and subdued them**: The Philistines had troubled Israel for centuries, and they often dominated the people of God. In the reign of David, he both **attacked** and **subdued** these troublesome enemies.

i. David didn't avoid fighting the Philistines because Israel had lost to them so many times before. "The thing that fascinates me about this complete victory is the utter contempt with which David treated the great power of his adversaries." (Redpath)

b. **David took Metheg Ammah**: This was another name for the famous Philistine city of Gath (compare 1 Chronicles 18:1). When David became king, the Philistines were *taking* territory from God's people. Under his leadership God's people began to take territory from the enemy.

2. (2) The Moabites put under tribute.

Then he defeated Moab. Forcing them down to the ground, he measured them off with a line. With two lines he measured off those to be put to death, and with one full line those to be kept alive. So the Moabites became David's servants, *and* brought tribute.

a. **He defeated Moab**: David's war against Moab and his harsh treatment of their army seemed out of place considering that David's great-grandmother was a Moabite (Ruth) and that he entrusted his mother and father into the care of the Moabites (1 Samuel 22:3-4). It may be that the Moabites killed or mistreated David's parents.

b. **Brought tribute**: God did not want Israel to *destroy* every neighbor nation. Generally, God wanted Israel to be so blessed and strong that other nations were "taxed" by Israel, thus recognizing their strength and dominance.

3. (3-8) David conquers a Syrian alliance.

David also defeated Hadadezer the son of Rehob, king of Zobah, as he went to recover his territory at the River Euphrates. David took from him one thousand *chariots,* seven hundred horsemen, and twenty thousand foot soldiers. Also David hamstrung all the chariot horses, except that he spared *enough* of them for one hundred chariots. When the Syrians of Damascus came to help Hadadezer king of Zobah, David killed twenty-two thousand of the Syrians. Then David put garrisons in Syria of Damascus; and the Syrians became David's servants, *and* brought tribute. The LORD preserved David wherever he went. And David took the shields of gold that had belonged to the servants of Hadadezer, and brought them to Jerusalem. Also from Betah and from Berothai, cities of Hadadezer, King David took a large amount of bronze.

a. **As he went to recover his territory at the River Euphrates**: The king of **Zobah** (a Syrian kingdom) ran into David on his way to capture territory to the Euphrates. David's dominance extended all the way to the Euphrates River.

i. "The border of Israel was carried to the line of the Euphrates, so that promise made by God to Abraham was fulfilled: 'Unto thy seed I have given this land, from the river of Egypt unto the great river, the river Euphrates.'" (Meyer)

ii. "Then there was Syria, the great heathen nation to the north, divided into two groups with capitals at Zobah and Damascus. They united together for protection but found themselves helpless against the might of David." (Redpath)

b. **David hamstrung all the chariot horses**: This was military necessity instead of mere animal cruelty. David could not care for so many horses while on military campaign and he could not give them back to the enemy.

c. **He spared enough of them for one hundred chariots**: That David kept such a small number shows remarkable self-control and trust in God. David obeyed the principle of Deuteronomy 17:15-16 and absolutely refused to trust in horses as military weapons. His trust was in God instead (Psalm 20:7 and 33:16-17).

d. **David took the shields of gold that had belonged to the servants of Hadadezer**: David took what was the glory of the enemy and transformed them into trophies of the power and goodness of God. Those **shields of gold** were set in the temple and testified to God's work in and through David.

    i. God loves to take people and things that are "trophies" for the Devil and make them trophies to His power and grace.

4. (9-14) The glory of David's kingdom.

When Toi king of Hamath heard that David had defeated all the army of Hadadezer, then Toi sent Joram his son to King David, to greet him and bless him, because he had fought against Hadadezer and defeated him (for Hadadezer had been at war with Toi); and *Joram* brought with him articles of silver, articles of gold, and articles of bronze. King David also dedicated these to the LORD, along with the silver and gold that he had dedicated from all the nations which he had subdued—from Syria, from Moab, from the people of Ammon, from the Philistines, from Amalek, and from the spoil of Hadadezer the son of Rehob, king of Zobah. And David made *himself* a name when he returned from killing eighteen thousand Syrians in the Valley of Salt. He also put garrisons in Edom; throughout all Edom he put garrisons, and all the Edomites became David's servants. And the LORD preserved David wherever he went.

a. **Toi sent Joram his son to King David, to greet him and bless him**: Neighboring nations saw the hand of God on David and brought him honor and gifts. They knew that a strong, godly leader of Israel was good for the whole community of nations, not just good for Israel itself.

    i. Not every pagan nation surrounding Israel was hostile to Israel or their God, and David did not treat them as if they were hostile. We make a mistake if we treat every unbeliever as an openly hostile enemy of the LORD.

b. **King David also dedicated these to the LORD**: When David received this acclaim from the nations he **dedicated** it all to the LORD. He knew that the praise and glory belonged to God, not himself. David could handle success as well as apparent failure.

c. **From Syria, from Moab, from the people of Ammon, from the Philistines, from Amalek**: By citing these subdued nations we learn that David's victories were complete. God used David to lead Israel to victory over enemies in every direction.

i. Israel possessed more of the land God promised to Abraham (Genesis 15:18-21) under David's reign than at any other time.

ii. David was able to accomplish so much against God's enemies because he, unlike Saul, was not consumed with fighting against the people of God.

d. **The LORD preserved David wherever he went**: This is the summary of this whole chapter. Every victory and every enemy subdued was a testimony to the LORD's preserving power in the life and reign of David.

B. David's administration.

1. (15) A general description of David's government.

So David reigned over all Israel; and David administered judgment and justice to all his people.

a. **So David reigned**: This chapter of victory, blessing, and prosperity describes the national life of Israel during the reign of David. This is one reason why he is generally regarded as the greatest king or ruler Israel ever had.

i. This is how God wanted to reign in the life of Saul, but Saul resisted the LORD and rejected His Spirit. Because David allowed God to subdue Him, the nations were subdued before David.

b. **David administered judgment and justice to all his people**: This shows that David was a great king to his own people, not only against neighboring nations. He fulfilled what is the fundamental duty of government - to administer **judgment and justice** (Romans 13:1-7).

2. (16-18) Key people in David's government.

Joab the son of Zeruiah *was* over the army; Jehoshaphat the son of Ahilud *was* recorder; Zadok the son of Ahitub and Ahimelech the son of Abiathar *were* the priests; Seraiah *was* the scribe; Benaiah the son of Jehoiada *was over* both the Cherethites and the Pelethites; and David's sons were chief ministers.

a. **Joab... Jehoshaphat... Zadok... Ahimelech... Seraiah... Benaiah**: No great ruler succeeds by himself. Only the smallest organizations are governed well without a gifted and committed team. Part of David's success as a ruler was found in his ability to assemble, train, empower, and maintain such a team.

i. We never find such a list regarding the organization of King Saul's government. This is because David's government had much more form and structure than Saul's.

ii. There is a limit to what we can be and what we can do for the LORD without order and organization. It isn't that order and organization are requirements for progress in the Christian life; they *are* progress in the Christian life, helping us become more like the LORD.

iii. *Nothing* is accomplished in God's kingdom without working through order and organization. While it may *seem* so, it is only an illusion. Behind the scenes God is moving with utmost order and organization though sometimes we cannot see it.

b. **The Cherethites and Pelethites**: These were hired soldiers from Crete. "By employing foreign guards to ensure the safety of the king David would minimize the possibility of becoming the victim of inter-tribal rivalries; these men from Crete could give whole-hearted allegiance to him." (Baldwin)

2 Samuel 9 - David's Kindness to Mephibosheth

A. David's kind heart towards the house of Saul.

1. (1) David's kind question.

Now David said, "Is there still anyone who is left of the house of Saul, that I may show him kindness for Jonathan's sake?"

a. **Is there still anyone who is left of the house of Saul**: In 1 Samuel 7 David asked, "What can I do for God?" and he proposed to build a temple for the Lord. Now David asked another question we should each ask: "What can I do for others?"

i. David's question showed a great love because Saul made himself an enemy of David. It was customary in those days for the king of a new dynasty to completely massacre anyone connected with the prior dynasty. David went against the principle of revenge and against the principle of self-preservation and asked what he could do for the family of *his enemy*.

b. **That I may show him kindness for Jonathan's sake**: David did this because he remembered his relationship and covenant with Jonathan (1 Samuel 20:14-15). His actions were not only based on feelings, but also on the promise of a covenant.

2. (2-4) Ziba, a former servant of Saul, tells David about Mephibosheth, son of Jonathan.

And *there was* a servant of the house of Saul whose name *was* Ziba. So when they had called him to David, the king said to him, "*Are* you Ziba?" And he said, "At your service!" Then the king said, "*Is* there not still someone of the house of Saul, to whom I may show the kindness of God?" And Ziba said to the king, "There is still a son of Jonathan *who is* lame in *his* feet." So the king said to him, "Where *is* he?" And Ziba said to the king, "Indeed he *is* in the house of Machir the son of Ammiel, in Lo Debar."

a. **Ziba**: David could only learn that there *was* a descendant of Saul still living and could only learn *where* he was through this servant named **Ziba**. This meant that Mephibosheth was in hiding.

b. **The kindness of God**: This phrase is key to understanding David's motivation in this chapter. David wanted to show someone else the same kindness God showed to him.

c. **There is still a son of Jonathan who is lame in his feet**: We first learned of Mephibosheth in 2 Samuel 4:4. It tells us that this son of Jonathan was made **lame in his feet** from an accident when they heard that his father Jonathan and his grandfather Saul died in battle.

> i. We should remember *why* Mephibosheth's nurse gathered the boy and fled in haste at the news of Saul and Jonathan's death. She rightly feared that the leader of a new royal dynasty would execute every potential heir of the former dynasty (2 Samuel 4:4).

d. **A son of Jonathan**: This means that according to the prior dynasty of Saul, Mephibosheth had the right to the throne. He was a son of the first-born son of the king, and other potential heirs were dead. In a political sense David could see Mephibosheth as a rival or a threat.

> i. Later in 2 Samuel 16:5-8 we see a man named Shimei who was a partisan for the house of Saul against David. There were at least a few in Israel who felt that the house of Saul should still reign over the nation and that David shouldn't be king. Mephibosheth might draw upon these partisans and develop a rival following.

> ii. Ishbosheth was Mephibosheth's uncle, and he waged a bloody war against David for the throne of Israel. There was at least an outside chance that Mephibosheth might do the same.

e. **He is in the house of Machir the son of Ammiel**: This speaks of Mephibosheth's low station in life. He didn't even have his own house. Instead, he lived in the house of another man.

> i. **Machir the son of Ammiel** later showed he was intensely loyal to David. When David's son Absalom led a rebellion against David, Machir supported and helped David at great danger to himself (2 Samuel 17:27-29).

B. David's kindness to Mephibosheth.

1. (5-6) Mephibosheth makes a humble appearance before David.

Then King David sent and brought him out of the house of Machir the son of Ammiel, from Lo Debar. Now when Mephibosheth the son of Jonathan, the son of Saul, had come to David, he fell on his face

and prostrated himself. Then David said, "Mephibosheth?" And he answered, "Here is your servant!"

a. **Then King David sent and brought him out of the house**: Mephibosheth must have been terrified when messengers from David knocked at his door and demanded that he come with them to see the king. In the back of his mind he anticipated the day when David would do as other kings did and massacre every potential rival to his throne.

i. The knock on the door also meant that Mephibosheth was no longer hidden from David. He felt secure as long as he believed the new king didn't know about him.

b. **He fell on his face and prostrated himself**: According to the custom of the times, Mephibosheth had a lot to fear from David. Yet his fear of David was not founded in fact, only on assumption.

i. Up to this point Mephibosheth and David never had a relationship, and it was because Mephibosheth wanted it that way. He avoided David out of unfounded fears.

2. (7-8) David removes the fears of Mephibosheth.

So David said to him, "Do not fear, for I will surely show you kindness for Jonathan your father's sake, and will restore to you all the land of Saul your grandfather; and you shall eat bread at my table continually." Then he bowed himself, and said, "What *is* your servant, that you should look upon such a dead dog as I?"

a. **Do not fear**: These words would be cruel or meaningless unless David gave Mephibosheth a *reason* to **not fear**.

b. **I will surely show you kindness for Jonathan your father's sake**: David made a covenant with Jonathan in 1 Samuel 20, promising to show kindness to the descendents of Jonathan. David gladly made good on his promise, though Jonathan was long dead.

c. **Will restore to you all the land of Saul**: David simply promised Mephibosheth would receive what was his. Mephibosheth knew about these lands all along, but he was afraid to take possession of them because it would expose him before the king. David went against all custom in showing such kindness to an heir of the former dynasty.

d. **And you shall eat bread at my table continually**: This went far beyond giving Mephibosheth what was rightly his. He gave Mephibosheth the honor of a close relationship with the king.

i. A similar promise is given to the followers of Jesus. Jesus told the disciples that they would eat and drink at His table in heaven (Luke 22:30).

e. **What is your servant, that you should look upon such a dead dog as I**: Mephibosheth didn't feel worthy of such generosity. He considered himself a **dead dog**, meaning a worthless and insignificant person.

i. All the years of hiding from the king and living in fear and poverty made Mephibosheth think of himself as worthless.

3. (9-12) David's instructions to Ziba.

And the king called to Ziba, Saul's servant, and said to him, "I have given to your master's son all that belonged to Saul and to all his house. You therefore, and your sons and your servants, shall work the land for him, and you shall bring in *the harvest,* **that your master's son may have food to eat. But Mephibosheth your master's son shall eat bread at my table always." Now Ziba had fifteen sons and twenty servants. Then Ziba said to the king, "According to all that my lord the king has commanded his servant, so will your servant do." "As for Mephibosheth,"** *said the king,* **"he shall eat at my table like one of the king's sons." Mephibosheth had a young son whose name** *was* **Micha. And all who dwelt in the house of Ziba** *were* **servants of Mephibosheth.**

a. **You therefore, and your sons and your servants, shall work the land for him**: In addition to the land, David gave Mephibosheth servants to work the land. The food from the land was for Mephibosheth's family, because he now ate at David's table.

b. **He shall eat at my table like one of the king's sons**: Mephibosheth was happy to know that David didn't want to kill him. To have a promise like this was almost unbelievable.

4. (13) David fulfills his promise to Mephibosheth.

So Mephibosheth dwelt in Jerusalem, for he ate continually at the king's table. And he was lame in both his feet.

a. **Mephibosheth dwelt in Jerusalem**: No longer hiding in fear of the king, this descendant of Saul now lived openly among the people of God.

b. **He ate continually at the king's table**: No longer in poverty and estranged from the king, now he had great privilege before the king.

c. **He was lame in both his feet**: Mephibosheth's weakness did not vanish. His life was far better, but he was still **lame**.

i. David's grace to Mephibosheth is a wonderful picture of God's grace to us. *We are Mephibosheth.*

- We are hiding, poor, weak, lame, and fearful before our King comes to us.
- We are separated from our King because of our wicked ancestors.
- We are separated from our King because of our deliberate actions.
- We separated ourselves from the King because we didn't know him or His love for us.
- Our King sought us out before we sought Him.
- The King's kindness is extended to us for the sake of another.
- The King's kindness is based on covenant.
- We must receive the King's kindness in humility.
- The King returns to us what we lost in hiding from Him.
- The King returns to us more than what we lost in hiding from Him.
- We have the privilege of provision at the King's table.
- We are received as sons at the King's table, with access to the King and fellowship with Him.
- We receive servants from the King.
- The King's honor does not immediately take away all our weakness and lameness, but it gives us a favor and standing that overcomes its sting and changes the way we think about ourselves.

ii. David's grace to Mephibosheth is also a pattern for us in serving and ministering to others. *We are David.*

- We should seek out our enemies and seek to bless them.
- We should look for the poor, weak, lame, and hidden to bless them.
- We should bless others when they don't deserve it, and bless them more than they deserve.
- We should bless others for the sake of someone else.
- We must show the *kindness of God* to others.

2 Samuel 10 - The War with the Ammonites and the Defeat of the Syrians

A. The offense of the Ammonites.

1. (1-2) David sends ambassadors to the Ammonites at the passing of their king.

It happened after this that the king of the people of Ammon died, and Hanun his son reigned in his place. Then David said, "I will show kindness to Hanun the son of Nahash, as his father showed kindness to me." So David sent by the hand of his servants to comfort him concerning his father. And David's servants came into the land of the people of Ammon.

> a. **I will show kindness**: David's kindness to Mephibosheth in the previous chapter didn't end his kind works. Here he showed kindness towards a pagan king because he sympathized with the loss of his father.

> b. **So David sent by the hand of his servants to comfort him**: David wasn't content to *feel* kindness towards Hanun. He *did* something to bring the grieving man comfort.

2. (3-5) Hanun, the new king of the Ammonites, treats Israel's ambassadors shamefully.

And the princes of the people of Ammon said to Hanun their lord, "Do you think that David really honors your father because he has sent comforters to you? Has David not *rather* sent his servants to you to search the city, to spy it out, and to overthrow it?" Therefore Hanun took David's servants, shaved off half of their beards, cut off their garments in the middle, at their buttocks, and sent them away. When they told David, he sent to meet them, because the men were greatly ashamed. And the king said, "Wait at Jericho until your beards have grown, and *then* return."

a. **Do you think that David really honors your father because he has sent comforters to you**: It's hard to explain why these advisers to Hanun said this to the king of Ammon. It's possible that they genuinely suspected David, or they perhaps used this as a way to appear wise and cunning to King Hanun. It is common for liars to always suspect others of lying.

b. **Hanun took David's servants, shaved off half of their beards, cut off their garments in the middle... and sent them away**: This was a disgraceful insult to these ambassadors from Israel. In that culture, many men would rather die than to have their beard shaved off. This was because a clean-shaven face was the mark of a slave and free men wore beards.

> i. "With the value universally set upon the beard by the Hebrews and other Oriental nations, as being man's greatest ornament, the cutting off of one-half of it was the greatest insult that could have been offered to the ambassadors, and through them to David their king." (Keil and Delitzsch)

> ii. "The *beard* is held in high respect in the East: the possessor considers it his greatest ornament; often swears by it; and, in matters of great importance, *pledges* it. Nothing can be more secure than a pledge of this kind; its owner will redeem it at the hazard of his life." (Clarke)

> iii. To **cut off their garments in the middle** was also an obvious insult and humiliation. "That the shame of their nakedness might appear, and especially that of their circumcision, so derided by the heathen." (Trapp)

> iv. To insult the ambassador is to insult the king. It was just as if they had done this to David himself. The same principle is true with King Jesus and His ambassadors. Jesus reminded His disciples: *If the world hates you, you know that it hated Me before it hated you.* (John 15:18)

c. **Wait at Jericho until your beards have grown, and then return**: David didn't use these men as political tools to whip up anger against the Ammonites. He cared more for their own dignity and honor and allowed them to wait before returning to Jerusalem.

3. (6-7) The Ammonites and Israelites prepare for war.

When the people of Ammon saw that they had made themselves repulsive to David, the people of Ammon sent and hired the Syrians of Beth Rehob and the Syrians of Zoba, twenty thousand foot soldiers; and from the king of Maacah one thousand men, and from Ish-Tob twelve thousand men. Now when David heard *of it*, he sent Joab and all the army of the mighty men.

a. **When the people of Ammon saw that they had made themselves repulsive**: They knew that *they* did this. David didn't reject the Ammonites; they **made themselves repulsive** to Israel.

b. **The people of Ammon sent and hired the Syrians**: This was a common practice in the ancient world. 1 Chronicles 19:6 says that the Ammonites paid 1,000 talents to the Syrians.

c. **When David heard of it, he sent Joab and all the army of the mighty men**: This is the first mention of David's **mighty men**, calling them the **army of the mighty men**. They formed a glorious fighting force, this army **of the mighty men**.

> i. It's important to understand that David was nothing without his mighty men, and they were nothing without him. He was their leader, but a leader is nothing without followers - and David had **an army of the mighty men** to follow him. These men didn't necessarily *start* as mighty men; many were the distressed, indebted, and discontent people who followed David at Adullam Cave (1 Samuel 22:1-2).

> ii. One of these mighty men was Adino the Eznite - famous for killing 800 men at one time (2 Samuel 23:8). Another was Jashobeam who killed 300 men at one time (1 Chronicles 11:11). Another was Benaiah who killed a lion in a pit on a snowy day and killed a huge Egyptian warrior with his own spear (1 Chronicles 11:22-23).

B. Victory for Israel.

1. (8-12) Joab divides the army into two groups.

Then the people of Ammon came out and put themselves in battle array at the entrance of the gate. And the Syrians of Zoba, Beth Rehob, Ish-Tob, and Maacah *were* by themselves in the field. When Joab saw that the battle line was against him before and behind, he chose some of Israel's best and put *them* in battle array against the Syrians. And the rest of the people he put under the command of Abishai his brother, that he might set *them* in battle array against the people of Ammon. Then he said, "If the Syrians are too strong for me, then you shall help me; but if the people of Ammon are too strong for you, then I will come and help you. Be of good courage, and let us be strong for our people and for the cities of our God. And may the LORD do *what is* good in His sight."

> a. **Joab saw that the battle line was against him before and behind**: As the army of the mighty men approached the Ammonite city, they found themselves surrounded. In front of them were the Ammonites **in battle array at the entrance of the gate**. Behind them were the Syrians **in the field**. It looked bad for the army of Israel.

b. **If the Syrians are too strong for me, then you shall help me**: Joab had only one strategy in battle - *attack*. Many generals would consider surrender when surrounded on both sides by the enemy, but not Joab. He called the army to courage and faith and told them to press on.

> i. "It is interesting to observe that in his arrangements he made no allowance for the possibility of ultimate defeat in his conflict with Ammon... it does not seem to have occurred to him that the combination might have been too much for both of them." (Morgan)

c. **Be of good courage, and let us be strong for our people and for the cities of our God. And may the LORD do what is good in His sight**: This is a great speech by Joab before the battle. He made at least three great points.

> i. **Be of good courage, and let us be strong**: Courage and strength are not matters of feeling and circumstance. They are matters of choice, especially when God makes His strength available to us. We can *be strong in the Lord and in the power of His might* (Ephesians 6:10).

> ii. **Let us be strong for our people and for the cities of our God**: Joab called them to remember *all they had to lose*. If they lost this battle they would lose both their **people** and their **cities**. This was a battle bigger than themselves, and the army of the mighty men had to remember that.

> iii. **And may the LORD do what is good in His sight**: Joab wisely prepared for the battle to the best of his ability and worked hard for the victory. At the same time, he knew that the outcome was ultimately in God's hands.

2. (13-14) Joab defeats the Syrians, and the Ammonites retreat to the city of Rabbah.

So Joab and the people who *were* with him drew near for the battle against the Syrians, and they fled before him. When the people of Ammon saw that the Syrians were fleeing, they also fled before Abishai, and entered the city. So Joab returned from the people of Ammon and went to Jerusalem.

a. **They fled before him**: It doesn't even say that Joab engaged the Syrians in battle. This mercenary army **fled before** the army of the mighty men because God was with them. God promised this kind of blessing upon an obedient Israel (Deuteronomy 28:7).

b. **They also fled before Abishai, and entered the city**: When the Ammonites saw the Syrians retreating, they also retreated. They could no more stand before the army of the mighty men than the Syrians could.

3. (15-19) David wipes out the Syrian reinforcements.

When the Syrians saw that they had been defeated by Israel, they gathered together. Then Hadadezer sent and brought out the Syrians who *were* beyond the River, and they came to Helam. And Shobach the commander of Hadadezer's army *went* before them. When it was told David, he gathered all Israel, crossed over the Jordan, and came to Helam. And the Syrians set themselves in battle array against David and fought with him. Then the Syrians fled before Israel; and David killed seven hundred charioteers and forty thousand horsemen of the Syrians, and struck Shobach the commander of their army, who died there. And when all the kings *who were* servants to Hadadezer saw that they were defeated by Israel, they made peace with Israel and served them. So the Syrians were afraid to help the people of Ammon anymore.

a. **When the Syrians saw that they had been defeated by Israel, they gathered together**: The enemies of Israel wouldn't quit after one defeat. They were a persistent enemy and came back to fight again.

b. **When it was told David, he gathered all Israel**: David gathered the rest of the army of Israel to prevent this army of Syrian reinforcements from crushing the army of the mighty men. The result was glorious: **the Syrians fled before Israel**.

i. The chapter ends with unfinished business at Rabbah. The offending Ammonites were still in their city and Joab returned to Jerusalem. In the Spring King David sent Joab and the army out again to deal with Rabbah as he waited in Jerusalem. While he waited comfortably in Jerusalem he fell into sin with Bathsheba.

ii. Many know about David's sin with Bathsheba, and how it happened when David waited in Jerusalem when he should have led the battle at Rabbah. 2 Samuel 10 shows that God gave David a warning by showing it necessary for him to come out against the Syrians. David *tried* to leave the battle with Joab in 2 Samuel 10, but his army *needed* him and God tried to show him that by blessing when David did go out to battle. 2 Samuel 10 was God's gracious warning that David sadly wasted.

2 Samuel 11 - David's Adultery and Murder

"In the whole of the Old Testament literature there is no chapter more tragic or full of solemn and searching warning than this." (G. Campbell Morgan)

A. David's adultery.

1. (1) David stays home from the war against the Ammonites.

It happened in the spring of the year, at the time when kings go out *to battle,* that David sent Joab and his servants with him, and all Israel; and they destroyed the people of Ammon and besieged Rabbah. But David remained at Jerusalem.

a. **In the spring of the year, at the time when kings go out to battle**: In that part of the world, wars were not normally fought during the winter months because rains and cold weather made travel and campaigning difficult. Fighting resumed in the spring.

b. **David sent Joab... But David remained at Jerusalem**: David should have been out at the battle, but he remained behind. In 2 Samuel 10 Joab and the army of the mighty men were preserved against the Syrians and the Ammonites, but they did not win a decisive victory. The decisive victory came when David led the battle at the end of 2 Samuel 10. Both through custom and experience God told David, "You need to be at the battle." **But David remained at Jerusalem**.

i. The principle of Galatians 5:16 rings true: *Walk in the Spirit, and you shall not fulfill the lust of the flesh.* If David had his attention where God wanted it, he would never put it where God *didn't* want it. "While Joab is busy in laying siege to Rabbah, Satan is to David, and far sooner prevailed." (Trapp)

ii. Nevertheless, it is wrong to think that *this* began the chain of events David followed all the way down to adultery and murder. David showed his disregard to God's plan for marriage many years before when he took more than one wife (1 Samuel 25:42-43, 2 Samuel 3:2-

5). David's practice of adding wives showed a lack of romantic restraint and an indulgence of his passions. *This* corrupt seed, sown long ago, grew unchecked long enough and would bear bitter fruit.

iii. "As I think of what happened, of this I am sure, that it did not happen all at once. This matter of Bathsheba was simply the climax of something that had been going on in his life for twenty years." (Redpath)

iv. Therefore, staying home from the battle merely provided *opportunity* for the long-standing lack of romantic restraint and indulgence of passion to display itself.

2. (2) David encounters temptation.

Then it happened one evening that David arose from his bed and walked on the roof of the king's house. And from the roof he saw a woman bathing, and the woman *was* very beautiful to behold.

a. **David arose from his bed and walked on the roof:** The Hebrew verb form of **walked** suggests that David paced back and forth on the roof. He couldn't sleep and was uneasy - uneasy because he wasn't where God wanted him to be.

b. **He saw a woman bathing:** There is little doubt that this woman (later called by the name *Bathsheba*) acted immodestly. Though it was **evening** and apparently the time when most people were asleep, *certainly* she knew that her bath was visible from the roof of the palace. Any immodesty on Bathsheba's part did not excuse David's sin, but she was still responsible for her wrong.

i. We must never be an occasion for sin in others, even in how we dress. Paul's word in 1 Timothy 2:9 is relevant here: *the women should adorn themselves in modest apparel, with propriety and moderation.*

c. **He saw a woman bathing:** David's sin was not in *seeing* Bathsheba. It was unlikely that he expected or planned to see her. David's sin was in *choosing* to keep his eyes on an alluring image after the sight came before his eyes.

i. Christians - men, especially - must learn to never let their eyes (or their mind) *rest* on alluring images except for what "belongs" to them in marriage. Our eyes must "bounce" off alluring images that come into sight.

ii. David's many wives did not satisfy his lust. This was because you can't *satisfy* lusts of the flesh, because they are primarily rebellious assertions of self. It wasn't so much that David wanted Bathsheba; it was that he would not be satisfied with what God gave him.

iii. The principle would be illustrated in an exaggerated way in the life of Solomon, David's son. Solomon had 700 wives and 300 concubines. David and Solomon show us that *if one woman isn't enough, 1000 women aren't enough.*

d. **The woman was very beautiful to behold**: Bathsheba's great beauty made the sight tempting. But the real strength of temptation often does not lie in the quality of the tempting object, but in the state of heart and mind of the one being tempted. David was carefully "prepared" to stumble at this very point. Even so, this temptation was not too strong for David, no matter how beautiful Bathsheba was.

i. For example, Joseph was more severely tempted to commit sexual immorality than David was here, but he fled that temptation.

ii. David looked at Bathsheba and said "beauty" but God saw this as *ugly*. The pleasures of sin deceive us like the bait hides the hook. We must call it what God calls it - sin. We want to say "affair" but God says "adultery." We want to say "love" but God says "lust." We want to say "sexy" but God says "sin." We want to say "romantic" but God says "ruin." We want to say "destiny" but God says "destruction."

3. (3) David pursues the temptation.

So David sent and inquired about the woman. And *someone* said, "Is this not Bathsheba, the daughter of Eliam, the wife of Uriah the Hittite?"

a. **So David sent and inquired**: David could have ended the temptation by leaving the scene at that time, even after entertaining the temptation for a while. Instead, David put himself into a *more* tempting situation.

b. **Is this not Bathsheba, the daughter of Eliam**: From this, David learned that the woman came from a notable family. She was from the upper classes. Her father was **Eliam**, one of David's Mighty Men (2 Samuel 23:34). Her grandfather was Ahithophel - one of David's chief counselors (2 Samuel 23:34, 2 Samuel 15:12).

c. **The wife of Uriah the Hittite**: From this, David learned that Bathsheba was married, and the wife of another of David's Mighty Men (2 Samuel 23:8, 39). He also learned that this woman's husband was away, because the Mighty Men were away in battle against the Ammonites. This knowledge made the situation far more tempting. David began to think, "I could get away with this."

i. David committed adultery in his heart up on the roof. Now he knows that he has an opportunity to commit adultery in practice. Adultery in the heart and mind is bad; adultery in practice is far worse.

ii. David should have received the news of the woman's identity as a warning. He learned that this woman was related to men close to David. In taking Bathsheba, David sinned against Uriah, Eliam, and Ahithophel - each man was close and important to David.

4. (4) David embraces the temptation.

Then David sent messengers, and took her; and she came to him, and he lay with her, for she was cleansed from her impurity; and she returned to her house.

a. **Then David sent messengers, and took her**: In this the man after God's heart went against his own heart, following through on a lustful impulse. David ignored every warning and way of escape God set before him.

i. "In the expression *he took her, and she came to him* there is no intimation whatever that David brought Bathsheba into his palace through craft or violence, but rather that she came at his request without any hesitation, and offered no resistance to his desires. Consequently Bathsheba is not to be regarded as free from blame." (Keil and Delitzsch)

ii. "We hear nothing of her reluctance, and there is no evidence that she was taken by force." (Clarke)

b. **He lay with her**: David *knew* this was wrong, yet he did it. It's hard to explain David's thinking here because he *wasn't* thinking. He acted on feeling and impulse instead of *thinking*.

i. If David *thought* about all this, he would see the cost was so much greater than he wanted to consider at the time. If David only knew theat this illicit pursuit of pleasure would directly or indirectly result in:

- An unwanted pregnancy.
- The murder of a trusted friend.
- A dead baby.
- His daughter raped by his son.
- One son murdered by another son.
- A civil war led by one of his sons.
- A son who imitates David's lack of self-control, leading him and much of Israel away from God.

ii. The same kind of ruin comes of adultery today. We think about all the children who went to bed without daddy at home because of the terrible attack on the United States on September 11, 2001. But far more children go to bed every night without daddy in the house because of adultery.

iii. At this moment David agreed with the world's understanding of the purpose of sex, seeing it primarily as the pursuit of a pleasurable experience. With his many wives, David may have *never* really understood *God's* purpose for sex: to be the "cement" that helps bond together a one-flesh relationship.

c. **She was cleansed from her impurity**: This confirms that Bathsheba had recently had her menstrual period and was not *already* pregnant when David committed adultery with her.

i. It *seemed* like David "got away" with this sin. But he and we could only think that if we believed the sin was something *good* God wanted to keep from David. David did something harmful and destructive to himself and others, and harm and destruction will come of it. Just because David wasn't caught at the moment doesn't mean that he got away with anything.

5. (5) Bathsheba's message to David.

And the woman conceived; so she sent and told David, and said, "I *am* with child."

a. **And the woman conceived**: David and Bathsheba didn't *plan* on this. They were terrified both at the "problem" of the pregnancy itself and that it meant that their adultery would be found out.

b. **So she sent and told David**: Her message "involved an appeal to him to take the necessary steps to avert the evil consequences of the sin, inasmuch as the law required that both the adulterer and adulteress should be put to death (Leviticus 20:10)." (Keil and Delitzsch)

B. David murders Uriah.

1. (6-11) David attempts to cover his sin.

Then David sent to Joab, *saying,* "Send me Uriah the Hittite." And Joab sent Uriah to David. When Uriah had come to him, David asked how Joab was doing, and how the people were doing, and how the war prospered. And David said to Uriah, "Go down to your house and wash your feet." So Uriah departed from the king's house, and a gift *of food* from the king followed him. But Uriah slept at the door of the king's house with all the servants of his lord, and did not go down to his

house. So when they told David, saying, "Uriah did not go down to his house," David said to Uriah, "Did you not come from a journey? Why did you not go down to your house?" And Uriah said to David, "The ark and Israel and Judah are dwelling in tents, and my lord Joab and the servants of my lord are encamped in the open fields. Shall I then go to my house to eat and drink, and to lie with my wife? *As you live, and as your soul lives,* I will not do this thing."

a. **Send me Uriah the Hittite**: When David heard the disastrous news of Bathsheba's pregnancy, he should have used it as a prompting to repent. Instead, David did what most unrepentant sinners do: he tried to hide his sin. He wanted to draw Uriah back home to have relations with Bathsheba to give a reason for her pregnancy.

i. The whole concept of hiding our sin is deceptive. Our sin is never hidden before God and only hidden with difficulty from our conscience. Our hidden sin hinders our fellowship with God and others and is a barrier to spiritual life and power.

ii. "The real question for us all is: Are we prepared to face sin? Not to discuss someone else's sin, but to face our own." (Redpath)

iii. The answer to hidden sin is confession and repentance. To whom should we confess? The answer is in the question, "Whom have we sinned against?" "If you sin secretly, confess secretly, admitting publicly that you need the victory but keeping details to yourself. If you sin openly confess openly to remove stumbling blocks from those whom you have hindered. If you have sinned spiritually (prayerlessness, lovelessness, and unbelief as well as their offspring, criticism, etc.) then confess to the church that you have been a hindrance." (J. Edwin Orr)

iv. "As soon as ever we are conscious of sin, the right thing is not to begin to reason with the sin, or to wait until we have brought ourselves into a proper state of heart about it, but to go at once and confess the transgression unto the Lord, there and then." (Spurgeon)

b. **David asked how Joab was doing, and how the people were doing, and how the war prospered**: This was David's awkward attempt to pretend that nothing happened. David gave every appearance that things were normal when before God nothing was normal or right.

c. **Go down to your house**: "David's design was that he should go and lie with his wife, that the child now conceived should pass for his, the honour of Bath-sheba be screened, and his own crime concealed. At this time he had no design of the murder of Uriah, nor of taking Bath-sheba to wife." (Clarke)

d. **The ark and Israel and Judah are dwelling in tents**: This shows that Uriah had a passion for the glory of God, even though he was a Hittite and not a native Jew.

e. **Shall I then go to my house to eat and drink, and to lie with my wife**: This shows Uriah as a man of great integrity. He was a true "team player" who did not want to enjoy the comforts of home as long as his fellow soldiers endured hardship on the field of battle.

   i. "David had expected and hoped that Uriah would prove to be like himself; instead he proved to be a man of integrity, whose first loyalty was to the king's interests rather than to his own pleasure." (Baldwin)

2. (12-13) David's second attempt to cover his sin fails.

Then David said to Uriah, "Wait here today also, and tomorrow I will let you depart." So Uriah remained in Jerusalem that day and the next. Now when David called him, he ate and drank before him; and he made him drunk. And at evening he went out to lie on his bed with the servants of his lord, but he did not go down to his house.

a. **Wait here today also, and tomorrow I will let you depart**: David lied to Uriah, knowing that he wanted to get back to the battle front as soon as possible. He hoped that Uriah would treat the coming evening as his last before returning to battle and be with Bathsheba.

b. **When David called him, he ate and drank before him**: David hoped that getting Uriah drunk would weaken his resolve to identify with his fellow troops. Yet Uriah **did not go down to his house**, refusing to enjoy what his fellow soldiers could not while the battle still raged.

   i. Uriah is a good example of how Christians should conduct themselves as fellow-soldiers in the spiritual battle. *Rejoice with those who rejoice, and weep with those who weep. Be of the same mind toward one another.* (Romans 12:15-16)

   ii. David was drunk with lust when he slept with Bathsheba; he hoped making Uriah drunk with wine would bring the same result.

c. **But he did not go down to his house**: Some commentators believe that Uriah suspected some infidelity in Bathsheba and avoided her out of jealousy. "It is like he smelt something." (Trapp)

3. (14-17) David sends Uriah to battle with his own death sentence in hand.

In the morning it happened that David wrote a letter to Joab and sent *it* by the hand of Uriah. And he wrote in the letter, saying, "Set Uriah in the forefront of the hottest battle, and retreat from him, that he may be struck down and die." So it was, while Joab besieged the city, that

he assigned Uriah to a place where he knew there *were* valiant men. Then the men of the city came out and fought with Joab. And *some* of the people of the servants of David fell; and Uriah the Hittite died also.

a. **David wrote a letter to Joab**: Meyer imagines Joab saying, "This master of mine can sing psalms with the best; but when he wants a piece of dirty work done, he must come to me."

b. **Set Uriah in the forefront of the hottest battle**: Having failed to cover his sin, David wanted Uriah dead. Many adulterers secretly wish death would free them to marry the object of their adultery. This is the very heart of murder even if the deed is not done. David had the power to act on his wish.

c. **And sent it by the hand of Uriah**: David trusted the integrity of Uriah so much that he made him the unwitting messenger of his own death sentence.

i. "This was the sum of treachery and villany. He made this most noble man the carrier of letters which prescribed the mode in which he was to be murdered." (Clarke)

d. **That he may be struck down and die**: David commanded Joab to arrange Uriah's death. Though it was hidden by the raging battle, Uriah was murdered just as surely as if David killed him in his own home.

i. "If a child was to be born, Uriah's lips, at least, should not be able to disown it." (Meyer)

ii. "David was better while a servant than when a king; for being a servant, he feared to kill Saul his adversary, but becoming a king, he basely slew his most faithful friend and dutiful subject." (Trapp)

iii. "Though we mourn over David's sin, yet we thank God that it was permitted, for if he had not so fallen he had not been able to help us when we are conscious of transgression. He could not have so minutely described our griefs if he had not felt the same. David lived, in this respect, for others as well as for himself." (Spurgeon)

e. **Uriah the Hittite died also**: Joab did exactly what David commanded. He knew it was wrong but simply followed orders and murdered Uriah at David's order.

i. If not immediately confronted, one sin can take a wretched course. David indulged his sensual lusts for years and ignored God's warnings and ways of escape. He allowed temptation to turn into lust and lust to turn into adultery. When the consequences of his adultery threatened to expose his sin, he covered it first with deception and then with murder. Satan could never tempt David with the entire package at once, but he deceived him with it piece by piece.

4. (18-25) Joab sends word of Uriah's death back to David.

Then Joab sent and told David all the things concerning the war, and charged the messenger, saying, "When you have finished telling the matters of the war to the king, if it happens that the king's wrath rises, and he says to you: 'Why did you approach so near to the city when you fought? Did you not know that they would shoot from the wall? Who struck Abimelech the son of Jerubbesheth? Was it not a woman who cast a piece of a millstone on him from the wall, so that he died in Thebez? Why did you go near the wall?'—then you shall say, 'Your servant Uriah the Hittite is dead also.'" So the messenger went, and came and told David all that Joab had sent by him. And the messenger said to David, "Surely the men prevailed against us and came out to us in the field; then we drove them back as far as the entrance of the gate. The archers shot from the wall at your servants; and *some* of the king's servants are dead, and your servant Uriah the Hittite is dead also." Then David said to the messenger, "Thus you shall say to Joab: 'Do not let this thing displease you, for the sword devours one as well as another. Strengthen your attack against the city, and overthrow it.' So encourage him."

a. **Who struck Abimelech the son of Jerubbesheth**: This is a reference to Judges 9:50-57, where Abimelech was killed by coming too close to the walls of a city under siege. The idea is that Joab knew it was a bad military move to get so close to the walls, but did it anyway on David's command.

b. **Uriah the Hittite is dead also**: David heard these words with relief. He thought that now he could marry Bathsheba and give a plausible explanation for her pregnancy.

c. **The sword devours one as well as another**: This was a proverb regarding fortunes of war. It was a way of saying, "These things happen." David said it to his own guilty conscience as much as he said it to Joab.

5. (26-27) David marries Bathsheba.

When the wife of Uriah heard that Uriah her husband was dead, she mourned for her husband. And when her mourning was over, David sent and brought her to his house, and she became his wife and bore him a son. But the thing that David had done displeased the LORD.

a. **When the wife of Uriah heard that Uriah her husband was dead**: We have no reason to believe that Bathsheba knew that David arranged the death of her husband. It is likely that David concealed all this from

Bathsheba. At the same time, she was partly relieved to hear of her husband's death.

i. "There is little doubt to be made but that she was inwardly glad, considering her danger of being punished an adulteress, and her hopes of being now made a queen." (Trapp)

b. **And she became his wife**: This was nothing new for David. He had added wives before, so now he simply added another.

i. "David is sort of a hero now, in the eyes of the people. He has taken into his harem, the poor, pregnant wife, the widow of one of his fallen captains, so that the people say, "My look at the way he stands behind his men! He takes care of their widows when they are killed in battle. My what a marvelous king!" (Smith)

c. **The thing that David had done displeased the LORD**: This is the first mention of God in the chapter. God witnessed every event and read the intent of every heart, but His displeasure is only implied until this specific statement.

i. David's state of heart in the intervening year is reflected in Psalm 32:1-5: *Blessed is he whose transgression is forgiven, whose sin is covered. Blessed is the man to whom the LORD does not impute iniquity, and in whose spirit there is no guile. When I kept silent, my bones grew old through my groaning all day long. For day and night Your hand was heavy upon me; my vitality was turned into the drought of summer. I acknowledged my sin to You, and my iniquity I have not hidden. I said, "I will confess my transgressions to the LORD," and You forgave the iniquity of my sin.*

ii. Psalm 32 shows that David was under intense conviction during this time and that all the joy in his life evaporated away. David knew the stress and agony of living a double, false life. He found no relief until he repented and got right with God again. "The better the man the dearer the price he pays for a short season of sinful pleasure." (Meyer)

iii. David was in that terrible place where he had too much sin in him to be happy in God, but he had too much of God in him to happy in sin. Because David was a man after God's heart, God drew David to repentance and restoration.

iv. "When there is the most necessity for confession, there is often the greatest tardiness in making it. It was so in David's case. . . I think I can see why he could not have gone straight away from the sin to confession, for the sin prevented the confession-the sin blinded the eye, stultified the conscience, and stupefied the entire spiritual nature of David." (Spurgeon)

2 Samuel 12 - Nathan Confronts David

A. Nathan's confrontation.

1. (1-4) Nathan's parable.

Then the LORD sent Nathan to David. And he came to him, and said to him: "There were two men in one city, one rich and the other poor. "The rich *man* had exceedingly many flocks and herds. But the poor *man* had nothing, except one little ewe lamb which he had bought and nourished; and it grew up together with him and with his children. It ate of his own food and drank from his own cup and lay in his bosom; and it was like a daughter to him. And a traveler came to the rich man, who refused to take from his own flock and from his own herd to prepare one for the wayfaring man who had come to him; but he took the poor man's lamb and prepared it for the man who had come to him."

> a. **Then the LORD sent Nathan to David**: David's sin displeased the LORD but David didn't listen to the conviction of the Holy Spirit or to his conscience. Now God sent someone else to speak to David. God mercifully kept speaking to David even when David didn't listen.
>
> > i. Yet no one should presume God will speak *forever* to the unrepentant sinner. God said in Genesis 6:3, *"My Spirit shall not strive with man forever."* When we hear or sense the conviction of the Holy Spirit, we must respond to it immediately, because it might not always be there.
>
> b. **There were two men in one city**: With wisdom and courage, Nathan used a story to get the message through to David. It was common in those days to keep a lamb as a pet, and Nathan used this story of the pet lamb to speak to his friend David.
>
> > i. Previously the prophet Nathan delivered a message of great blessing to David (2 Samuel 7). David knew that Nathan was not a negative critic but a friend. It made David receptive to the message of the story.

c. **Who refused to take from his own flock... he took the poor man's lamb**: The sin Nathan describes is *theft*. There is a sense in which David *stole* something from Uriah. The Bible (in 1 Corinthians 7:3-5) says that in marriage a husband has authority over the body of his wife (and vice-versa). Obviously, David did not have this authority over the body of Bathsheba and he *stole* from Uriah. Adultery and sexual immorality are *theft* - taking something that does not belong to us.

> i. This principle is also true regarding pornography and lust. Leviticus 18 describes the sin of *uncovering the nakedness* of those other than our spouse. The idea is that the nakedness of others doesn't belong to us, and it is theft if we take it.

2. (5-6) David condemns the cruel man of Nathan's story.

So David's anger was greatly aroused against the man, and he said to Nathan, "As the LORD lives, the man who has done this shall surely die! And he shall restore fourfold for the lamb, because he did this thing and because he had no pity."

a. **David's anger was greatly aroused**: Nathan did not ask David for a judicial decision, and David naturally assumed the story was true. David immediately passed sentence on the guilty man of Nathan's story. David showed that we often try to rid our guilty consciences by passing judgment on someone else.

b. **The man who has done this shall surely die**: David's sense of righteous indignation was so affected by his own guilt that he commanded a death sentence for the hypothetical case brought by Nathan, even though it wasn't a capital crime.

> i. David had to condemn his own sin before he could find forgiveness. We often try to find refuge in excusing or minimizing or deflecting the blame of our sin; we simply do not condemn sin in ourselves.

> ii. David's use of the oath "**As the LORD lives**" shows how passionate his indignation is. He called God to witness the righteousness of his death sentence upon Nathan's hypothetical rich man.

c. **He shall restore fourfold for the lamb**: David rightly knew that penalizing the rich man - even with death - wasn't enough. He also had to **restore** something to the man he took something from. David knew that true repentance means *restitution*.

> i. **Restore fourfold** also shows that David's sin and hardness of heart did not diminish his *knowledge* of the Bible. He immediately knew what the Bible said about those who steal sheep: *If a man steals an ox or a sheep, and slaughters it or sells it, he shall restore five oxen for an ox*

and four sheep for a sheep (Exodus 22:1). David knew the words of the Bible but was distant from the Author.

d. **Because he had no pity**: The idea is that the man *should* have had pity on his neighbor and did not. In the same way David *should* have had pity on Uriah and Bathsheba's father and grandfather.

3. (7-9) Nathan's confrontation.

Then Nathan said to David, "You *are* the man! Thus says the LORD God of Israel: 'I anointed you king over Israel, and I delivered you from the hand of Saul. I gave you your master's house and your master's wives into your keeping, and gave you the house of Israel and Judah. And if *that had been* too little, I also would have given you much more! Why have you despised the commandment of the LORD, to do evil in His sight? You have killed Uriah the Hittite with the sword; you have taken his wife *to be* your wife, and have killed him with the sword of the people of Ammon.'"

a. **You are the man**: With this, Nathan applied the parable with alarming simplicity. Nathan had to shock David into seeing his sin for what it was. "This was downright plain dealing indeed." (Trapp)

i. Shocked, but not frightened: "You cannot frighten men into repentance, you may frighten them into remorse; and the remorse may or may not lead on to repentance." (Maclaren)

ii. "God accuses us and condemns us one by one that He may save us one by one." (Maclaren) A *personal* salvation requires a *personal* conviction of sin. It wasn't enough for David to confess that he was a sinner in a general sense; he had to confess his sin at this very point.

iii. In this sense, the confession of our sin needs to be specific. J. Edwin Orr tells of a time of revival in Brazil when a lady stood in a crowded church and said, "Please pray for me. I need to love people more." The leader gently told her, "That is not confession, sister. Anyone could have said it." Later in the service the woman stood again and said, "Please pray for me. What I should have said is that my tongue has caused a lot of trouble in this church." Her pastor whispered to the leader, "Now she's talking."

iv. It costs nothing to say, "I'm not everything I should be" or "I ought to be a better Christian." It does cost something to say, "I have been a trouble-maker in this church" or "I have had bitterness towards certain leaders, to whom I apologize right now."

b. **I anointed you... I delivered you... I gave you... and gave you the house of Israel and Judah... I also would have given you much more**:

Through Nathan, God explained to David that his sin was really a base expression of *ingratitude*. When God gave all this to David and had so much more to give him, David sought out sin instead.

c. **Why have you despised the commandment of the LORD, to do evil in His sight**: In Psalm 19:8, David said: *The commandment of the LORD is pure, enlightening the eyes.* Yet by his sin he **despised the commandment of the LORD**. David acted as if God's command was wrong and to be **despised** when he did **evil in His sight**.

d. **You have killed Uriah... you have taken his wife**: This is another way of saying, "**You are the man!**" God won't allow David to blame anyone or anything else.

4. (10) David's punishment.

"Now therefore, the sword shall never depart from your house, because you have despised Me, and have taken the wife of Uriah the Hittite to be your wife."

a. **The sword shall never depart from your house**: God promised that from that day forward David would know violence and bloodshed among his own family members.

i. David demanded fourfold restitution for the man in Nathan's parable. God exacted fourfold restitution for Uriah from four of David's sons: Bathsheba's child, Amnon, Absalom, and Adonijah.

b. **Because you have despised Me**: In 2 Samuel 12:9 God said that David *despised the commandment of the LORD.* Here Nathan explained that in doing this, David **despised** God Himself. We can't despise God's commandments without despising Him.

i. Many who live in either open or hidden sin seem to believe it has no effect or little effect on their relationship with God. But despising God's commandment means despising God Himself, and we can't have fellowship with God and despise Him at the same time. *If we say that we have fellowship with Him, and walk in darkness, we lie and do not practice the truth.* (1 John 1:6)

c. **The wife of Uriah the Hittite**: God didn't even use Bathsheba's own name. He wanted David to consider Bathsheba not only as an individual but also as **the wife of Uriah the Hittite**.

5. (11-12) Adversity against David.

"Thus says the LORD: 'Behold, I will raise up adversity against you from your own house; and I will take your wives before your eyes and give *them* to your neighbor, and he shall lie with your wives in the sight of

this sun. For you did *it* secretly, but I will do this thing before all Israel, before the sun.'"

a. **I will raise up adversity against you from your own house**: The Living Bible translates **adversity** as "rebellion." God warned David that because he troubled another man's house, God will allow trouble to come upon David's house - from within the house.

b. **I will take your wives before your eyes and give them to your neighbor**: As David violated another man's wife, so another will violate his wives. This was fulfilled in 2 Samuel 16:21-22.

i. "Absalom abused his father's concubines on the house-top: and haply on that same terrace from whence he first looked, liked, and lusted after Bath-sheba." (Trapp)

c. **You did it secretly, but I will do this thing before all Israel**: In these judgments, David will reap what he has sown - with interest.

B. David's repentance; the death of his newborn son.

1. (13a) David's repentance.

So David said to Nathan, "I have sinned against the LORD."

a. **I have sinned against the LORD**: David's confession is a good example. He placed the blame squarely on his own shoulders. He did not minimize his offence. David realized that he especially sinned against God.

i. In the original Hebrew, David's statement **I have sinned against the LORD** amounts to only two words: *hata al-Yahweh*. These two words, and the heart they reflect, show the fundamental difference between David and Saul. Confession doesn't need to be long to be real and sincere. "The greatest griefs are not always the most verbal. Saul confessed his sin more largely, but less effectually." (Trapp)

ii. "The words are very few, but that is a good sign of a thoroughly broken spirit. There is no excuse, no hiding, no concealment of the sin. There is no searching for a loophole, no pretext put forward, no human weakness pleaded. He acknowledged his guilt openly, candidly and without any denial of truth." (Keil and Delitzsch)

iii. This was an exceptionally good response from a man of David's standing in life. When confronted with sin, kings often say, "Off with their head." David showed that God was working on his heart all along, and Nathan's confrontation was just the last piece of that work.

iv. "In all this David was pre-eminently revealed as a man after God's own heart. Other men who had been guilty of such failure might have defended their actions, might have slain the prophet. Not so with this man. He knew God, and he knew the wrong of his action, and he confessed his sin." (Morgan)

b. **I**: David spoke of *himself*. It isn't "we" though it was true that he was not the only sinner. Yet David knew that he had to deal with *his* sin. David showed *personal responsibility* for his sin.

c. **Have sinned**: David didn't use elaborate or soft vocabulary. He **sinned**. It wasn't a *mistake*, an *error*, a *mess-up*, an *indiscretion*, or a *problem*.

d. **Against the LORD**: This expressed the *enormity* of David's sin. His sin against Bathsheba, against Uriah, against Ahithophel, against his wives and children, and against the nation were great. But his sin **against the LORD** was greatest of all. There are no small sins against a great God, and great sins are even greater.

e. **I have sinned against the LORD**: After meditation, David more eloquently expressed his repentance in Psalm 51.

> i. *Have mercy upon me, O God, according to Your lovingkindness; according to the multitude of Your tender mercies, blot out my transgressions. Wash me thoroughly from my iniquity, and cleanse me from my sin. For I acknowledge my transgressions, and my sin is ever before me. Against You, You only have I sinned, and done this evil in Your sight - that You may be found just when You speak, and blameless when You judge.... For You do not desire sacrifice, or else I would give it; You do not delight in burnt offering. The sacrifices of God are a broken spirit, and a broken and contrite heart - these, O God, You will not despise.* (Psalm 51:1-4; 16-17)

> ii. David's awareness of sin, desire for cleansing, recognition of God's righteous judgment, and understanding of what God wants are each clear in Psalm 51.

2. (13b-14) Forgiveness and the immediate consequences of David's sin.

And Nathan said to David, "The LORD also has put away your sin; you shall not die. However, because by this deed you have given great occasion to the enemies of the LORD to blaspheme, the child also *who is* born to you shall surely die."

a. **The LORD also has put away your sin**: God's forgiveness was *immediate*. God did not demand a time of probation. **You shall not die** meant that David would be spared the penalty for adultery commanded under the Law of Moses.

> i. David believed the word of the prophet, "*You are the man!*" Therefore he could also believe the word, "**The LORD also has put away your sin; you shall not die.**"

b. **You have given great occasion to the enemies of the** LORD **to blaspheme**: David did this by doing just what those **enemies of the** LORD would do in the same situation. What David did was not unusual among the kings and rulers of the world, but it should be unusual among God's people.

  i. "Hitherto all the king's care had been to conceal his sin from the world, which yet he could not do with all his skill, for the enemies had got it by the end." (Trapp)

c. **The child who is born to you shall surely die**: There is a difference in judgment *for* sin and judgment *by* sin. God forgave David's sin, but He would not shield him from every consequence of the sin. David had to face the consequences of his sin, beginning with the death of the child born by Bathsheba.

  i. This shows that God didn't only want to heal David of the *guilt* of his sin; He also wanted to heal David of the *presence* of this sin. We never read of David committing adultery again because God used these chastisements to drive such impurities far from David.

  ii. "Long before his sin with Bathsheba, there were various indications as to David's special liability to temptation. That sin only threw out upon the surface the evil that was always within him; and now God, having him see that the deadly cancer is there, begins to use the knife to cut it out of him." (Spurgeon)

3. (15-23) The death of David's son.

Then Nathan departed to his house. And the LORD **struck the child that Uriah's wife bore to David, and it became ill. David therefore pleaded with God for the child, and David fasted and went in and lay all night on the ground. So the elders of his house arose *and went* to him, to raise him up from the ground. But he would not, nor did he eat food with them. Then on the seventh day it came to pass that the child died. And the servants of David were afraid to tell him that the child was dead. For they said, "Indeed, while the child was alive, we spoke to him, and he would not heed our voice. How can we tell him that the child is dead? He may do some harm!" When David saw that his servants were whispering, David perceived that the child was dead. Therefore David said to his servants, "Is the child dead?" And they said, "He is dead." So David arose from the ground, washed and anointed himself, and changed his clothes; and he went into the house of the** LORD **and worshiped. Then he went to his own house; and when he requested, they set food before him, and he ate. Then his servants said to him, "What *is* this that you have done? You fasted and wept for the child *while he***

was alive, but when the child died, you arose and ate food." And he said, "While the child was alive, I fasted and wept; for I said, 'Who can tell *whether* the LORD will be gracious to me, that the child may live?' But now he is dead; why should I fast? Can I bring him back again? I shall go to him, but he shall not return to me."

a. **The LORD struck the child**: This is hard for many to accept. Sadly, often the innocent suffers because of the sin of the guilty. Since the sickness came immediately after the words of Nathan the prophet, it was received as from the hand of God.

    i. "The biblical writer does not hesitate to attribute directly to the Lord the sickness of this child, in accordance with the prophet's word." (Baldwin)

    ii. This was far more tragic for David and Bathsheba than it was for the child himself. Their young son suffered for several days and we may trust that God's comfort was extended to the child in the midst of suffering. At the end of his suffering, the child went to eternal glory. Though the child died, the chastisement was really upon David and Bathsheba and not upon the child.

    iii. "God's mercy to his erring and repentant children will be shown in converting the results of their sin into the fires of their purification." (Meyer)

    iv. This illustrates an important principle: *even when sin is forgiven a price must be paid.* God does not simply pass over or excuse our sin. It is forgiven, and a price is paid. Often *an innocent party* pays the price for forgiveness.

b. **That Uriah's wife bore to David**: Though Uriah was dead, and David was legally married to Bathsheba, the Biblical writer still refered to Bathsheba as **Uriah's wife**. This is because when the child was conceived Uriah was alive and Bathsheba was **Uriah's wife**. It is God's way of saying, "Uriah's death and the subsequent marriage *doesn't* make everything alright."

c. **David therefore pleaded with God for the child**: David was right to take the announcement of God's judgment as an invitation to earnestly seek His mercy. When God's judgment is announced or present, we shouldn't receive it passively or fatalistically. We should cry out to God in repentance and ask for His grace and mercy.

d. **David fasted... the child died**: This shows that extraordinary prayer and fasting does not change God's mind. It put David in the right place to receive what he must from God, but it did not "force" God to change His plan.

i. Extraordinary prayer and fasting are not tools to get whatever we want from God. They are demonstrations of radical submission and surrender to God's power and will.

e. **He went into the house of the LORD and worshiped**: This shows that David's extraordinary prayer and fasting were answered. He had a sense of peace when the child died, knowing he did all he could to seek God's mercy in a time of chastisement.

i. The ability to worship and honor God in a time of trial or crisis is a wonderful demonstration of spiritual confidence.

f. **I shall go to him, but he shall not return to me**: David was confident that his son would meet him in heaven. This is an indication that babies and perhaps children who pass from this world to the next will go to heaven.

i. 1 Corinthians 7:14 is an additional promise of assurance that the children of believers are saved, at least until they come to an age of personal accountability (which may differ for each child). However, we have no similar *promise* for the children of parents who are not Christians.

ii. If the children of non-Christian parents are saved and do go to heaven – even some of them – it is important to understand that it is not because they are *innocent*. As sons and daughters of guilty Adam, we are also born guilty. If such children go to heaven, it is not because they are innocent and *deserve* heaven, but because the rich mercy of God has been extended to them also.

4. (24-25) God extends His mercy to David and Bathsheba.

Then David comforted Bathsheba his wife, and went in to her and lay with her. So she bore a son, and he called his name Solomon. Now the LORD loved him, and He sent *word* by the hand of Nathan the prophet: So he called his name Jedidiah, because of the LORD.

a. **David comforted Bathsheba his wife**: This is the first time the Biblical writer called this woman **Bathsheba** except for the mere reporting of her name in 2 Samuel 11:3. Each time before this she is called *the wife of Uriah*. Only now, after the chastisement for sin, is she called **Bathsheba his wife**.

b. **Went in to her and lay with her**: This shows that God did not command that David forsake or leave Bathsheba, even though his marriage to her was originally sinful. He was to honor God in the marriage commitment he made, even though it began in sin.

i. Paul commands the same principle in 1 Corinthians 7:17: *As the Lord has called each one, so let him walk*. In part, this principle in context warns us against trying to undo the past in regard to relationships. God tells us to repent of whatever sin is there and then to move on. If you are married to your second wife, after wrongfully divorcing your first wife, and become a Christian, don't think you must now leave your second wife and go back to your first wife, trying to undo the past. As the Lord has called you, walk in that place right now.

c. **So she bore a son... the LORD loved him**: Here is the great forgiveness and tenderness of God. He did not hold a grudge against David and Bathsheba. The days of blessing and fruitfulness were not over for David.

i. "David's best sons came of Bath-sheba; because they were the fruit of their humiliation." (Trapp)

d. **He called his name Solomon**: Remarkably it is *this son* - the son born out of a marriage that began in adultery - that will be heir to David's throne. God chose this son among David's many sons to be heir to the throne and the ancestor of the Messiah to demonstrate the truth that *God forgives repentant sinners.*

i. People may not forgive; we may refuse to really believe that we are forgiven. But God forgives repentant sinners.

e. **So he called his name Jedidiah**: The name **Jedidiah** means, "loved of the LORD." It was God's way of saying that He would love and bless this son of David and Bathsheba.

C. David's victory at Rabbah.

1. (26-28) Joab fights against Rabbah.

Now Joab fought against Rabbah of the people of Ammon, and took the royal city. And Joab sent messengers to David, and said, "I have fought against Rabbah, and I have taken the city's water *supply.* Now therefore, gather the rest of the people together and encamp against the city and take it, lest I take the city and it be called after my name."

a. **Joab fought against Rabbah and the people of Ammon, and took the royal city**: This continued the war that began in 2 Samuel 10. Joab was about to complete the defeat of the Ammonites.

b. **Lest I take the city and it be called after my name**: Joab goaded David into returning to battle by saying, "I'll take all the credit to myself if you don't come and finish this war."

i. Joab struggled for more than a year to conquer Rabbah, and the victory only came when David got things right with God. There was an unseen spiritual reason behind the lack of victory at Rabbah.

ii. "David's sin at home had hindered Joab's good success abroad, and retarded the conquest of this city Rabbah, which now is ready to be taken, that David reconciled to God may have the honour of it." (Trapp)

2. (29-31) David captures the city, takes the spoil, and sets the people to forced labor.

So David gathered all the people together and went to Rabbah, fought against it, and took it. Then he took their king's crown from his head. Its weight *was* a talent of gold, with precious stones. And it was *set* on David's head. Also he brought out the spoil of the city in great abundance. And he brought out the people who *were* in it, and put *them to work* with saws and iron picks and iron axes, and made them cross over to the brick works. So he did to all the cities of the people of Ammon. Then David and all the people returned to Jerusalem.

a. **David gathered all the people together and went to Rabbah**: This was the final phase of David's restoration. He went back to doing what he should have done all along - leading Israel out to battle, instead of remaining in Jerusalem.

b. **Fought against it, and took it**: David was in victory once again. His sin did not condemn him to a life of failure and defeat. There was chastisement for David's sin, but it did not mean that his life was ruined.

c. **He took their king's crown... it was set on David's head**: David's sin didn't take away his crown. Had David refused the voice of Nathan the Prophet it might have. Because David responded with confession and repentance, there was sill a crown for **David's head**.

i. "David's fall should put those who have not fallen on their guard, and save from despair those who have." (Augustine)

2 Samuel 13 - Amnon, Tamar, and Absalom

A. Amnon and Tamar.

1. (1-2) Amnon's infatuation with Tamar.

After this Absalom the son of David had a lovely sister, whose name *was* Tamar; and Amnon the son of David loved her. Amnon was so distressed over his sister Tamar that he became sick; for she *was* a virgin. And it was improper for Amnon to do anything to her.

> a. **Absalom the son of David had a lovely sister, whose name was Tamar**: This brother and sister were the children of David through his wife *Maacah*, who was *the daughter of Talmai, king of Geshur* (2 Samuel 3:3).

> b. **Amnon the son of David**: Amnon was David's first-born son, born from his wife *Ahinoam the Jezreelitess* (2 Samuel 3:2). Being the first born, Amnon was the crown prince - first in line for the throne of Israel.

> c. **Amnon the son of David loved her**: Amnon longed for Tamar so much that he became lovesick. It was even more difficult for him because **she was a virgin** - meaning that she was available for marriage, but not to Amnon because marriage between half-brother and half-sister was forbidden.

>> i. The name **Tamar** means "Palm Tree," signifying fruitfulness. The name **Absalom** means "His Father's Peace." The name **Amnon** means "Faithful, Stable." "None of them answered their names." (Trapp)

2. (3-5) Jonadab's evil advice.

But Amnon had a friend whose name *was* Jonadab the son of Shimeah, David's brother. Now Jonadab *was* a very crafty man. And he said to him, "Why *are* you, the king's son, becoming thinner day after day? Will you not tell me?" Amnon said to him, "I love Tamar, my brother Absalom's sister." So Jonadab said to him, "Lie down on your bed and pretend to be ill. And when your father comes to see you, say to him, 'Please let my sister Tamar come and give me food, and prepare the food in my sight, that I may see *it* and eat it from her hand.'"

a. **Jonadab was a very crafty man**: Indeed, he was. His wicked advice to Amnon began a disastrous chain of events. **Jonadab** was a cousin to Amnon, being the son of David's brother (2 Samuel 13:32).

> i. "A friend no friend; a carnal friend, a spiritual enemy, who advised, for the recovery of the body, the ruin of his soul." (Trapp)

b. **I love Tamar**: As later events will show, he did not **love Tamar** at all. Amnon lusted after Tamar and called it love. He certainly was not the last person to do this, and lust often masquerades as love.

c. **My brother Absalom's sister**: If Absalom was **my brother** then clearly Tamar was *my sister*. In his lust, Amnon did not allow himself to call Tamar his sister - instead, she was **Absalom's sister**. The power of lust is strong enough to twist the way we see reality.

d. **Lie down on your bed and pretend to be ill**: Jonadab advised Amnon to deceitfully arrange a private meeting with Tamar. He didn't need to say, "And then force yourself on Tamar," because in their shared wickedness, Jonadab and Amnon thought the same wicked thoughts.

3. (6-10) Amnon pretends illness in order to be alone with Tamar.

Then Amnon lay down and pretended to be ill; and when the king came to see him, Amnon said to the king, "Please let Tamar my sister come and make a couple of cakes for me in my sight, that I may eat from her hand." And David sent home to Tamar, saying, "Now go to your brother Amnon's house, and prepare food for him." So Tamar went to her brother Amnon's house; and he was lying down. Then she took flour and kneaded *it,* made cakes in his sight, and baked the cakes. And she took the pan and placed *them* out before him, but he refused to eat. Then Amnon said, "Have everyone go out from me." And they all went out from him. Then Amnon said to Tamar, "Bring the food into the bedroom, that I may eat from your hand." And Tamar took the cakes which she had made, and brought *them* to Amnon her brother in the bedroom.

a. **Please let Tamar my sister come and make a couple of cakes for me**: Amnon's behavior was clearly childish, and David indulged it. Amnon acted like a baby. It is childish to refuse food unless it is served the way we want it.

> i. From this and other passages, it appears that David was generally indulgent towards his children. This may be because he felt guilty that in having so many wives, children, and responsibilities of state, he didn't take the time to be a true father to his children. He dealt with the guilt by being soft and indulgent with his children.

ii. Amnon took Jonadab's wicked advice quickly and completely. It's too bad that men don't often respond to godly advice the same way.

b. **And David sent home to Tamar**: This was what Amnon wanted. If he was alone with Tamar because David commanded it, then it gave part of the responsibility to David.

c. **But he refused to eat**: Amnon showed by this that everything he told David was a lie. He continued the deception, so he could force himself upon Tamar in the bedroom.

4. (11-14) Amnon rapes Tamar.

Now when she had brought *them* to him to eat, he took hold of her and said to her, "Come, lie with me, my sister." And she answered him, "No, my brother, do not force me, for no such thing should be done in Israel. Do not do this disgraceful thing! And I, where could I take my shame? And as for you, you would be like one of the fools in Israel. Now therefore, please speak to the king; for he will not withhold me from you." However, he would not heed her voice; and being stronger than she, he forced her and lay with her.

a. **Come, lie with me, my sister**: Amnon's evil naturally revealed itself. Here he admitted his incestuous desire as he made the wicked suggestion to Tamar. Amnon seems to be a spoiled prince who always took what he wanted.

b. **Do not do this disgraceful thing**: Tamar easily saw how evil and **disgraceful** this was. Amnon could not see what was so plainly evident because he was blinded by lust.

c. **Where could I take my shame? And as for you, you would be like one of the fools in Israel**: Tamar wisely asked Amnon to consider the result of his desire, both for her and for him. It would **shame** Tamar and reveal Amnon as **one of the fools**. Blinded by lust, Amnon would not see the inevitable result of his desire.

i. "There is something exceedingly tender and persuasive in this speech of Tamar; but Amnon was a mere brute, and it was all lost on him." (Clarke)

d. **Please speak to the king; for he will not withhold me from you**: The Law of Moses commanded against any marriage between a half-brother and half-sister (Leviticus 18:11). Tamar probably said this simply as a ploy to get away from Amnon.

e. **He forced her and lay with her**: This was nothing but rape. Tamar did whatever she could to avoid this and all the blame clearly rests on Amnon.

5. (15) Amnon rejects Tamar.

Then Amnon hated her exceedingly, so that the hatred with which he hated her *was* greater than the love with which he had loved her. And Amnon said to her, "Arise, be gone!"

a. **Amnon hated her exceedingly**: This revealed Amnon's attraction for Tamar for what it was - lust, not love. Amnon was attracted to Tamar for what he could get from her, not out of concern for her. In many lustful relationships there is a combination of both love and lust but in Amnon's attraction there was only lust.

i. In this single-minded lust, Amnon only built upon the example of his father David. David was never *this* dominated by lust, but he was pointed in the same direction. David's multiple marriages (2 Samuel 3:2-5) and his adultery with Bathsheba (2 Samuel 11:2-4) displayed this same direction.

ii. This is often how *the iniquity of the fathers* is carried on by *the children to the third and fourth generations* (Exodus 20:5). A child will often model a parent's sinful behavior and will often go further in the direction of sin the parent is pointed towards.

b. **The hatred with which he hated her was greater than the love with which he had loved her**: Amnon had no real love for Tamar, only lust - and so he immediately felt guilty over his sin. Tamar was simply a reminder of his foolish sin. He wanted every reminder of his sin to be put far away.

i. "Let me give a friendly, fatherly tip unto all of you young girls, who may be in the position of Tamar, in that you have some fellow who is really pressing hard to have sex with you. He is the soul of kindness. He is very attentive. He calls all the time. He opens the door for you. He brings you flowers, but he's pushing hard for a sexual relationship. Don't give in. If you really love him, make him wait until you're married. If he really loves you, he will. Over, and over, time and again, the fellow will press and press until he has taken you to bed, and that's the last you see or hear from him. You're no longer a challenge. He's conquered, and he's off for new conquests. If you really love him and want him, make him wait. If you really love God, and love yourself, make him wait." (Smith)

6. (16-18) Amnon casts Tamar out of his presence.

So she said to him, "No, indeed! This evil of sending me away *is* worse than the other that you did to me." But he would not listen to her. Then he called his servant who attended him, and said, "Here! Put this *woman*

out, away from me, and bolt the door behind her." Now she had on a robe of many colors, for the king's virgin daughters wore such apparel. And his servant put her out and bolted the door behind her.

a. **This evil of sending me away is worse than the other that you did to me**: What Amnon did to Tamar was wrong, but he could still *somewhat* redeem the situation by either marrying her or paying her bride-price in accordance with Exodus 22:16-17 and Deuteronomy 22:28-29. The payment was meant to compensate for the fact that Tamar was now less likely to be married because she was no longer a virgin.

b. **A robe of many colors**: The idea behind the Hebrew phrase is that it was a robe extending all the way down to the wrists and ankles, as opposed to a shorter one. It was a garment of privilege and status, showing the person did not have to work much.

c. **Put this woman out... bolt the door behind her**: Tamar deserved better treatment as an *Israelite*. Tamar deserved better treatment as a *relative*. Tamar deserved better treatment as a *sister*. Tamar deserved better treatment as a *princess*. Despite all this, Amnon spitefully treated Tamar as **this woman**.

7. (19-20) Tamar mourns, Absalom comforts her.

Then Tamar put ashes on her head, and tore her robe of many colors that *was* on her, and laid her hand on her head and went away crying bitterly. And Absalom her brother said to her, "Has Amnon your brother been with you? But now hold your peace, my sister. He *is* your brother; do not take this thing to heart." So Tamar remained desolate in her brother Absalom's house.

a. **Tamar put ashes on her head, and tore her robe**: Tamar correctly treated this as a calamity and did not hide the truth that a terrible crime was committed against her. She did not give place to the voice of shame saying, "This was somehow your fault."

b. **Has Amnon your brother been with you**: Amnon probably thought he had concealed his crime. Nevertheless, it was so obvious to Absalom that he immediately knew that Amnon was responsible.

i. Part of the blindness of lust leads the lustful man or woman to believe that his or her actions are not obviously apparent to others. Amnon was deceived by this blindness of lust.

ii. Tamar didn't go to her father David because she knew he tended to be indulgent to his sons, and he excused all kinds of evil in them.

8. (21-22) David's anger and inaction.

But when King David heard of all these things, he was very angry. And Absalom spoke to his brother Amnon neither good nor bad. For Absalom hated Amnon, because he had forced his sister Tamar.

a. **When King David heard of all these things, he was very angry**: David was right to be angry, but he didn't *do* anything to either protect Tamar or to correct Amnon. It may be that David was conscious of his own guilt in a similar matter and therefore felt a lack of moral authority to discipline his own son.

    i. If this was the case, it was a grave miscalculation on David's part. He could have said to Amnon, "I know the evil that results when we don't restrain our lusts and affections. This is something you must address and conquer in God's strength." "Why did he not reprove him at least very sharply for this foul fact?" (Trapp)

    ii. "They say a man never hears his own voice till it comes back to him from the phonograph. Certainly a man never sees the worst of himself until it reappears in his child." (Meyer)

b. **Absalom spoke to his brother Amnon neither good nor bad**: Absalom played it cool. His devious nature set the stage for future revenge. "Nothing is more unsafe to be trusted, than the fair looks of a festered heart." (Trapp)

B. Absalom murders Amnon.

1. (23-27) Absalom invites all the king's sons to a feast.

And it came to pass, after two full years, that Absalom had sheepshearers in Baal Hazor, which *is* near Ephraim; so Absalom invited all the king's sons. Then Absalom came to the king and said, "Kindly note, your servant has sheepshearers; please, let the king and his servants go with your servant." But the king said to Absalom, "No, my son, let us not all go now, lest we be a burden to you." Then he urged him, but he would not go; and he blessed him. Then Absalom said, "If not, please let my brother Amnon go with us." And the king said to him, "Why should he go with you?" But Absalom urged him; so he let Amnon and all the king's sons go with him.

a. **After two full years**: Two years went by but Absalom did not stop plotting the revenge of Amnon's sin against Tamar.

b. **Absalom had sheepshearers in Baal Hazor**: Sheep shearing was a festive time, and it was natural that Absalom had a great feast and invited **Amnon and all the king's sons**.

c. **So he let Amnon and all the king's sons go with him**: Absalom showed some of the same cunning we saw in Amnon. He asked *David* to allow

Amnon and all the king's sons to come to the feast. This made David partly responsible for their meeting, just as Amnon got David to allow Tamar to visit him with food.

2. (28-29) Absalom kills Amnon.

Now Absalom had commanded his servants, saying, "Watch now, when Amnon's heart is merry with wine, and when I say to you, 'Strike Amnon!' then kill him. Do not be afraid. Have I not commanded you? Be courageous and valiant." So the servants of Absalom did to Amnon as Absalom had commanded. Then all the king's sons arose, and each one got on his mule and fled.

a. **When Amnon's heart is merry with wine**: As a cunning killer, Absalom waited until Amnon was relaxed and vulnerable. Amnon probably came to the feast nervous about being with Absalom, but after a few cups of wine he was relaxed. At that moment, Absalom gave the order to "**Strike Amnon!**" and they murdered him.

b. **So the servants of Absalom did to Amnon as Absalom had commanded**: God promised David that *the sword shall never depart from your house* (2 Samuel 12:10) in judgment of David's sin. This is definitely a partial fulfillment of this promise.

i. "As David had committed adultery, made Uriah drunk, and then murdered him: so Amnon committeth incest, is made drunk, and [is] then murdered." (Trapp)

3. (30-36) David learns of the murder of Amnon.

And it came to pass, while they were on the way, that news came to David, saying, "Absalom has killed all the king's sons, and not one of them is left!" So the king arose and tore his garments and lay on the ground, and all his servants stood by with their clothes torn. Then Jonadab the son of Shimeah, David's brother, answered and said, "Let not my lord suppose they have killed all the young men, the king's sons, for only Amnon is dead. For by the command of Absalom this has been determined from the day that he forced his sister Tamar. Now therefore, let not my lord the king take the thing to his heart, to think that all the king's sons are dead. For only Amnon is dead." Then Absalom fled. And the young man who was keeping watch lifted his eyes and looked, and there, many people were coming from the road on the hillside behind him. And Jonadab said to the king, "Look, the king's sons are coming; as your servant said, so it is." So it was, as soon as he had finished speaking, that the king's sons indeed came, and they lifted up their voice and wept. Also the king and all his servants wept very bitterly.

a. **Absalom has killed all the king's sons, and not one of them is left**: It is significant that David did not react to this news with disbelief. He sensed that Absalom was capable of such evil. David reacted with mourning instead of disbelief.

b. **Let not my lord suppose they have killed all the young men**: Jonadab brought the "good" news to David that **only Amnon is dead**, and dead because he **forced his sister Tamar**. Jonadab probably hoped to gain favor with David by bringing this more favorable news, but God knew that Jonadab set the whole course of events in motion with his wicked advice to Amnon (2 Samuel 13:3-5).

c. **The king and all his servants wept very bitterly**: David is rightly grieved at learning of the death of his eldest son, the Crown Prince Amnon. Yet David's lack of correction against Amnon contributed to this murder. If David had administered Biblical correction according to Exodus 22:16-17 and Deuteronomy 22:28-29, Absalom would not have felt so free to administer his own brutal correction.

  i. "Absalom's fratricide would never have taken place if David had taken instant measures to punish Amnon." (Meyer)

4. (37-39) Absalom flees to Geshur.

But Absalom fled and went to Talmai the son of Ammihud, king of Geshur. And *David* mourned for his son every day. So Absalom fled and went to Geshur, and was there three years. And King David longed to go to Absalom. For he had been comforted concerning Amnon, because he was dead.

a. **Absalom fled and went to Talmai the son of Ammihud, king of Geshur**: Absalom did not go to a city of refuge because he was guilty, and the cities of refuge were only meant to protect the *innocent*.

b. **Absalom fled and went to Geshur**: This made sense for Absalom because his mother's father was the king of Geshur (2 Samuel 3:3).

c. **King David longed to go to Absalom**: After three years, the sting of Amnon's murder was not as sharp. David simply longed to be reconciled to Absalom again - without correcting his son for his evil. David's indulgence towards Amnon is repeated towards Absalom and he will meet a similar end.

2 Samuel 14 - Absalom Returns to Jerusalem

A. Joab intercedes for Absalom.

1. (1-3) Joab's plan to reconcile David and Absalom.

So Joab the son of Zeruiah perceived that the king's heart *was* concerned about Absalom. And Joab sent to Tekoa and brought from there a wise woman, and said to her, "Please pretend to be a mourner, and put on mourning apparel; do not anoint yourself with oil, but act like a woman who has been mourning a long time for the dead. Go to the king and speak to him in this manner." So Joab put the words in her mouth."

a. **Joab the son of Zeruiah perceived that the king's heart was concerned about Absalom**: David was obviously troubled by his estranged relationship with Absalom. Joab, David's chief general, **perceived** this and decided to do something to bring David and Absalom back together.

i. "In the case of Absalom and the king, the relationship remained virtually deadlocked, neither side having the spiritual incentive to break it." (Baldwin)

ii. We know that Joab was fiercely loyal to David, and he may have done this to protect David. Joab figured that it was dangerous to have Absalom stewing away in a distant country and felt that the safest thing to do was to bring about reconciliation between father and son.

b. **Joab sent to Tekoa and brought from there a wise woman**: Joab decided to soften David's heart towards Absalom by bringing a widow before him with a similar story of estrangement from her son.

2. (4-11) The woman of Tekoa tells a story of one son dead and another son threatened with death.

And when the woman of Tekoa spoke to the king, she fell on her face to the ground and prostrated herself, and said, "Help, O king!" Then the king said to her, "What troubles you?" And she answered, "Indeed I *am*

a widow, my husband is dead. Now your maidservant had two sons; and the two fought with each other in the field, and *there was* no one to part them, but the one struck the other and killed him. And now the whole family has risen up against your maidservant, and they said, 'Deliver him who struck his brother, that we may execute him for the life of his brother whom he killed; and we will destroy the heir also.' So they would extinguish my ember that is left, and leave to my husband *neither* name nor remnant on the earth." Then the king said to the woman, "Go to your house, and I will give orders concerning you." And the woman of Tekoa said to the king, "My lord, O king, *let* the iniquity *be* on me and on my father's house, and the king and his throne *be* guiltless." So the king said, "Whoever says *anything* to you, bring him to me, and he shall not touch you anymore." Then she said, "Please let the king remember the LORD your God, and do not permit the avenger of blood to destroy anymore, lest they destroy my son." And he said, *"As* the LORD lives, not one hair of your son shall fall to the ground."

a. **Help, O king**: In ancient Israel those who felt that their local judges didn't treat them fairly had access to the court of the king himself.

b. **Deliver him who struck his brother, that we may execute him for the life of his brother whom he killed**: The woman of Tekoa referred to the custom of the *avenger of blood*. The *avenger of blood* had the responsibility of avenging the death of a member of the family.

i. The *cities of refuge* mentioned in Numbers 35:9-34 were meant to protect someone guilty of manslaughter from being killed by an avenger of blood before the case could be heard properly.

c. **As the LORD lives, not one hair of your son shall fall to the ground**: This was what the woman - and Joab behind her - waited to hear. In saying this, David ignored the cause of justice for the sake of family sympathy and loyalty. In personal relationships it is a good and glorious thing to be generous with forgiveness and mercy when we are wronged. But David had a responsibility as the king and chief judge of Israel, and when he was sorely tempted to neglect that responsibility he did neglect it.

i. "He guaranteed safety at the expense of justice, and immediately the farsighted woman captured him in her trap." (Redpath)

ii. Several factors made this woman's appeal successful.

- She was a widow, which would invite sympathy.
- She lived at some distance from Jerusalem, which made it difficult to easily know or inquire of the facts of her case.
- She was old, which gave more dignity to her story.

- She wore the clothes of mourning to heighten the effect.

- She brought a case of family estrangement to David.

- She brought a case that was not too similar, lest it arouse David's suspicions.

3. (12-17) The woman of Tekoa applies her story to David and Absalom.

Therefore the woman said, "Please, let your maidservant speak *another* word to my lord the king." And he said, "Say on." So the woman said: "Why then have you schemed such a thing against the people of God? For the king speaks this thing as one who is guilty, *in that* the king does not bring his banished one home again. For we will surely die and *become* like water spilled on the ground, which cannot be gathered up again. Yet God does not take away a life; but He devises means, so that His banished ones are not expelled from Him. Now therefore, I have come to speak of this thing to my lord the king because the people have made me afraid. And your maidservant said, 'I will now speak to the king; it may be that the king will perform the request of his maidservant. For the king will hear and deliver his maidservant from the hand of the man *who would* destroy me and my son together from the inheritance of God.' Your maidservant said, 'The word of my lord the king will now be comforting; for as the angel of God, so *is* my lord the king in discerning good and evil. And may the LORD your God be with you.'"

a. **The king does not bring his banished one home again**: The woman of Tekoa spoke boldly to David, confronting his sin of not initiating reconciliation with Abasalom. Because he was estranged from David and growing more and more bitter, Absalom was a threat to Israel and David allowed it (**Why then have you schemed such a thing against the people of God?**).

i. David had some responsibility to *initiate* reconciliation. If David approached Absalom, he might be rejected, but he still had the responsibility to try. Yet as king and chief judge of Israel, he also had a responsibility to both initiate reconciliation and to do it the right way. David will not succeed in this.

ii. "He is willing to pardon the meanest of his subjects the murder of a brother at the instance of a poor widow, and he is not willing to pardon his son Absalom, whose restoration to favour is the desire of the whole nation." (Clarke)

b. **We will surely die and become like water spilled on the ground**: The woman of Tekoa wisely spoke to David about the *urgency* of reconciliation.

"David, we all die and then the opportunity for reconciliation is over. Do it now."

c. **But He devises means, so that His banished ones are not expelled from Him**: The woman of Tekoa meant, "Find a way to do it, David. God finds a way to bring us back to Himself." It is true that God finds a way - but not at the expense of justice. God reconciles us by *satisfying* justice, not by *ignoring* justice.

> i. This is one of the best gospel texts in the Old Testament. If we are under the chastening of God, we may feel like **banished ones**. Yet we can put our place of being **His banished ones**, belonging to Him and trusting Him to bring us back to Him.

> ii. God has devised a way to bring the banished back to Him, that they might not be **expelled from Him**. The way is through the person and work of Jesus, and how He stood in the place of guilty sinners as He hung on the cross and received the punishment that we deserved.

4. (18-20) David asks the woman of Tekoa if Joab prompted her.

Then the king answered and said to the woman, "Please do not hide from me anything that I ask you." And the woman said, "Please, let my lord the king speak." So the king said, *"Is* the hand of Joab with you in all this?" And the woman answered and said, *"As* you live, my lord the king, no one can turn to the right hand or to the left from anything that my lord the king has spoken. For your servant Joab commanded me, and he put all these words in the mouth of your maidservant. To bring about this change of affairs your servant Joab has done this thing; but my lord *is* wise, according to the wisdom of the angel of God, to know everything that *is* in the earth."

> a. **Is the hand of Joab with you in all this**: David somehow knew that a plan this subtle had to come from the **hand of Joab**.

> b. **He put all these words in the mouth of your maidservant**: Joab orchestrated this with precision. He knew exactly what strings to pull in David. Joab was loyal to David, but it was not a selfless loyalty.

5. (21-24) Absalom returns to Jerusalem but not to David.

And the king said to Joab, "All right, I have granted this thing. Go therefore, bring back the young man Absalom." Then Joab fell to the ground on his face and bowed himself, and thanked the king. And Joab said, "Today your servant knows that I have found favor in your sight, my lord, O king, in that the king has fulfilled the request of his servant." So Joab arose and went to Geshur, and brought Absalom to Jerusalem.

And the king said, "Let him return to his own house, but do not let him see my face." So Absalom returned to his own house, but did not see the king's face.

a. **Bring back the young man Absalom**: Joab got what he wanted and what he thought was best for the nation of Israel. He hoped that Absalom's reconciliation with David would prevent a rebellion.

b. **Let him return to his own house, but do not let me see my face**: David was overindulgent with his sons in the past (as when he got angry but did nothing against Amnon in 2 Samuel 13:21). Now David is too harsh with Absalom, refusing to see him after he had been in exiled in Geshur for three years (2 Samuel 13:38).

i. When parents don't discipline properly from the beginning, they tend to overcompensate in the name of "toughness." This often provokes the children to wrath (Ephesians 6:4) and makes the parent-child relationship worse.

B. Absalom gains an audience with his father.

1. (25-27) Absalom's handsome appearance.

Now in all Israel there was no one who was praised as much as Absalom for his good looks. From the sole of his foot to the crown of his head there was no blemish in him. And when he cut the hair of his head—at the end of every year he cut *it* because it was heavy on him—when he cut it, he weighed the hair of his head at two hundred shekels according to the king's standard. To Absalom were born three sons, and one daughter whose name *was* Tamar. She was a woman of beautiful appearance.

a. **In all Israel there was no one who was praised as much as Absalom for his good looks**: This begins to explain why Absalom was popular in Israel. Israel was attracted to King Saul because he was a very good-looking man (1 Samuel 9:2).

i. Absalom was also a man of political destiny. He was the third son of David (2 Samuel 3:2-5). The firstborn Amnon was gone, and we hear nothing more of Chileab, the second born. It is likely that Absalom was the *crown prince*, next in line for the throne.

b. **He weighed the hair of his head at two hundred shekels**: Absalom had such a great head of hair that he cut five and one-half pounds of hair off his head every year.

i. "He was extremely proud of his long hair, and he lost his life because of it." (Redpath)

c. **One daughter whose name was Tamar**: Absalom was a man of deep and sympathetic feeling. He memorialized his wronged sister Tamar by naming a daughter after her.

2. (28-32) Absalom is refused audience with the king.

And Absalom dwelt two full years in Jerusalem, but did not see the king's face. Therefore Absalom sent for Joab, to send him to the king, but he would not come to him. And when he sent again the second time, he would not come. So he said to his servants, "See, Joab's field is near mine, and he has barley there; go and set it on fire." And Absalom's servants set the field on fire. Then Joab arose and came to Absalom's house, and said to him, "Why have your servants set my field on fire?" And Absalom answered Joab, "Look, I sent to you, saying, 'Come here, so that I may send you to the king, to say, "Why have I come from Geshur? *It would be* better for me *to be* there still."' Now therefore, let me see the king's face; but if there is iniquity in me, let him execute me."

a. **Absalom dwelt two full years in Jerusalem, but did not see the king's face**: During these two years we can imagine that Absalom grew more and more bitter against David. He was reconciled but only partially. David offered only a partial, incomplete reconciliation.

i. Absalom was banished from Israel because he murdered his brother Amnon (2 Samuel 13). Yet Absalom felt entirely justified in killing the man who raped his sister. His sense of justification made the bitterness against David more intense.

b. **Joab's field is near mine, and he has barley there; go and set it on fire**: Frustrated that he could not see his father, Absalom burnt Joab's fields to get his attention. This showed how brutal and amoral Absalom was.

i. It's hard to think of a greater contrast than that between Absalom and the Prodigal Son of Jesus' parable. The Prodigal Son came back humble and repentant. Absalom came back burning Joab's fields.

ii. At the same time, sometimes God gets *our* attention by setting our "barley field" on fire. "He, knowing that we will not come by any other means, sendeth a serious trial - he sets our barley-field on fire, which he has a right to do, seeing our barley-fields are far more his than they are ours." (Spurgeon)

c. **If there is any iniquity in me, let him execute me**: This statement reflects Absalom's sense that he was fully justified in what he did.

3. (33) David receives Absalom.

So Joab went to the king and told him. And when he had called for Absalom, he came to the king and bowed himself on his face to the ground before the king. Then the king kissed Absalom.

a. **So Joab went to the king and told him**: As brutal and amoral as Absalom was, it worked. Burning Joab's fields got his attention and made Joab intercede on Absalom's behalf.

b. **He came to the king and bowed himself on his face to the ground**: Absalom outwardly submits to David, but David's two-year refusal to reconcile left a legacy of bitterness in Absalom that turned out badly for David, for Absalom, and for Israel.

c. **Then the king kissed Absalom**: David offered Absalom forgiveness without any repentance or resolution of the wrong. In personal relationships it is often a sign of love and graciousness to overlook a wrong. Proverbs 10:12 says, *Hatred stirs up strife, but love covers all sins.* But as King of Israel this was more than a personal matter with David. He was the "chief judge" of Israel and David excused and overlooked Absalom's obvious crimes.

i. "He should have kicked him rather; and not have hardened him to further villainy." (Trapp)

ii. "David's forgiveness of Absalom was completely inadequate, leading to a further outbreak of sin. God's forgiveness of a man's soul is completely adequate, and a great deterrent to continued sin." (Redpath)

iii. "May God write it on your soul: if the pardon you want is that God should wink at your sin, He will not do it." (Redpath)

2 Samuel 15 - Absalom's Rebellion

A. Absalom's deceptive take-over.

1. (1-6) Absalom steals the hearts of the men of Israel.

After this it happened that Absalom provided himself with chariots and horses, and fifty men to run before him. Now Absalom would rise early and stand beside the way to the gate. So it was, whenever anyone who had a lawsuit came to the king for a decision, that Absalom would call to him and say, "What city *are* you from?" And he would say, "Your servant *is* from such and such a tribe of Israel." Then Absalom would say to him, "Look, your case *is* good and right; but *there is* no deputy of the king to hear you." Moreover Absalom would say, "Oh, that I were made judge in the land, and everyone who has any suit or cause would come to me; then I would give him justice." And *so* it was, whenever anyone came near to bow down to him, that he would put out his hand and take him and kiss him. In this manner Absalom acted toward all Israel who came to the king for judgment. So Absalom stole the hearts of the men of Israel.

> a. **Chariots and horses, and fifty men to run before him**: This means that Absalom did not want the chariot for speed, but to make an impressive procession. This was Absalom the politician, sensing what the people wanted and knowing how to give them the image of it.

> > i. Samuel - who anointed Absalom's father - never went around with horses and chariots and an entourage. Samuel traveled on foot - and as a man, *Absalom wasn't worthy to be mentioned in the same breath as Samuel.*

> b. **Whenever anyone who had a lawsuit came to the king for a decision**: Ancient kings were more than the heads of government, they were also the "supreme court" of their kingdom. If someone believed that a local court did not give them justice, they then appealed to the court of the king, where the king or a representative of the king heard their case.

c. **Your case is good and right; but there is no deputy of the king to hear you**: Absalom stirred up dissatisfaction with David's government and campaigned against David by promising to provide justice that David (supposedly) denied the people.

d. **Oh, that I were made judge in the land... I would give him justice**: Absalom had reason to be disillusioned with David's administration of justice. When Amnon raped Tamar, David did nothing. When Absalom did something about it, David banished Absalom and kept him at a distance even when he came back.

e. **Whenever anyone came near to bow down to him, that he would put out his hand and take him and kiss him**: Absalom was skilled at projecting a "man of the people" image. In an obvious display, he wouldn't let others **bow down** to him but would lift them up, shake their hand, and embrace them.

i. From what we know of Absalom, we can guess that he really didn't consider himself a "man of the people" at all. He regularly acted as if he was above others and the laws that applied to others didn't apply to him. He knew he was better looking, better connected, better off, and had better political instincts than most anyone. But these political instincts made Absalom know that he had to create the *image* of a man of the people.

ii. In ancient Israel they were too easily impressed by image and too slow to see or appreciate the reality behind the image. Since the days of ancient Israel, we have only become *more* impressed by image over reality.

iii. "Absalom appeared to be the *real* and was the *undisputed* heir to the throne; David could not, in the course of nature, live very long; and most people are more disposed to hail the beams of the *rising*, than exult in those of the *setting*, sun." (Clarke)

f. **Absalom stole the hearts of the men of Israel**: Absalom's cunning campaign worked. He became more *popular* and more *trusted* than David.

i. Absalom knew exactly how to do this.

- He carefully cultivated an exciting, enticing image (**chariots and horses, and fifty men to run before him**).

- He worked hard (**Absalom would rise early**).

- He knew where to position himself (**beside the way to the gate**).

- He looked for troubled people (**anyone who had a lawsuit**).

- He reached out to troubled people (**Absalom would call to him**).

- He took a personal interest in the troubled person (**What city are you from?**).

- He sympathized with the person (**your case is good and right**).

- He never attacked David directly (**no deputy of the king to hear you**).

- He left the troubled person more troubled (**no deputy of the king to hear you**).

- Without directly attacking David, Absalom promised to do better. (**Oh, that I were made judge in the land, and everyone who has any suit or cause would come to me; then I would give him justice.**)

ii. Absalom's clever approach made him able to subvert and divide David's kingdom without saying any specific thing that could condemn him. If someone objected Absalom would simply say, "Tell me one specific thing that I have said or done." In fact, Absalom could do all this and say, "I'm *helping* David to deal with all this discontent" while Absalom was in fact *promoting* discontent.

iii. David was Israel's greatest king - and Israel became dissatisfied with him and let a wicked, amoral man steal their hearts. There are many reasons why this happened.

- David was getting older.

- David's sins diminished his standing.

- People like change and Absalom was exciting.

- Absalom was very skilled and cunning.

- David had to enter into the *fellowship of His sufferings*, and be rejected like the Son of David would later be rejected.

iv. "Behold a king, the greatest that ever lived, a profound politician, an able general, a brave soldier, a poet of the most sublime genius and character, a prophet of the Most High God, and the deliverer of his country, driven from his dominions by his own son, abandoned by his fickle people." (Clarke)

v. We might say that Absalom's greatest sin was *impatience*. Absalom "seemed to stand *nearest to the throne*; but his sin was, that he sought it during his father's life, and endeavoured to dethrone him in order to sit in his stead." (Clarke)

2. (7-10) Absalom plans the overthrow of David's kingdom.

Now it came to pass after forty years that Absalom said to the king, "Please, let me go to Hebron and pay the vow which I made to the LORD. For your servant took a vow while I dwelt at Geshur in Syria, saying, 'If the LORD indeed brings me back to Jerusalem, then I will serve the LORD.'" And the king said to him, "Go in peace." So he arose and went to Hebron. Then Absalom sent spies throughout all the tribes of Israel, saying, "As soon as you hear the sound of the trumpet, then you shall say, 'Absalom reigns in Hebron!'"

a. **After forty years**: This perhaps was Absalom's age at the time, but some believe that this is a minor corruption of the text and that it should read *four years* based on the readings in Syriac and Arabic translations, Josephus, and some Hebrew manuscripts.

b. **Let me go to Hebron and pay the vow which I made to the LORD**: Absalom committed treason under the guise of worship. He knew that the *appearance* of spirituality could work in his favor.

i. It is possible - perhaps likely - that Absalom did all this *feeling* spiritual and in God's will. Men in Absalom's place often deceive themselves with words like this: "Lord, You know we need new leadership. Thank you for raising me up for such a time as this. Guide me and bless me, O Lord, as I endeavor to do what is best for Your people."

ii. Divisive people almost *never* see themselves as divisive. They see themselves as crusaders for God's righteous cause and often believe or hope God's hand is upon them. This is especially a problem when many will only believe a person is divisive if they were to *admit* they are divisive.

c. **Go in peace**: Ironically, these were David's last words to Absalom. Upon hearing these, Absalom went to carry on the plot to overthrow David's kingdom.

d. **Absalom reigns in Hebron**: Absalom counted on the hope that most of Israel would see this as *succession* and not *treason*.

3. (11-12) Legitimacy for Absalom's government.

And with Absalom went two hundred men invited from Jerusalem, and they went along innocently and did not know anything. Then Absalom sent for Ahithophel the Gilonite, David's counselor, from his city—from Giloh—while he offered sacrifices. And the conspiracy grew strong, for the people with Absalom continually increased in number.

a. **With Absalom went two hundred men invited from Jerusalem**: Absalom wisely knew that he needed others to endorse - or at least to *appear* to endorse - his government. He counted on these **two hundred men** who were not *against* David to at least be silent and therefore give the impression that they were *for* Absalom.

i. When the innocent and unknowing are among the divisive, their *silence* is always received as *agreement.*

b. **Absalom sent for Ahithophel the Gilonite, David's counselor**: Absalom's government gained more prestige when one of David's top aides defected to his side. This genuinely hurt David; he described his feelings in Psalm 41: *Even my own familiar friend in whom I trusted, who ate my bread, has lifted up his heel against me* (Psalm 41:9).

i. Ahithophel was renowned for his wisdom and wise counsel (2 Samuel 16:23). Even wise men can take their side with divisive and destructive leaders. In Ahithophel's case it was probably prompted by a sense of personal hurt and bitterness because of what David did to Ahithophel's granddaughter Bathsheba (2 Samuel 11:3 and 23:34).

c. **While he offered sacrifices**: Absalom was careful to keep up his religious practices, both for the sake of image and because he was deceived enough to think that God wanted to bless him.

d. **And the conspiracy grew strong**: Once some started coming to Absalom's side, it encouraged more and more to come. Momentum for division builds because others are doing it.

B. David escapes with the help of faithful friends.

1. (13-18) David flees from Jerusalem.

Now a messenger came to David, saying, "The hearts of the men of Israel are with Absalom." So David said to all his servants who *were* with him at Jerusalem, "Arise, and let us flee; or we shall not escape from Absalom. Make haste to depart, lest he overtake us suddenly and bring disaster upon us, and strike the city with the edge of the sword." And the king's servants said to the king, "We *are* your servants, *ready to do* whatever my lord the king commands." Then the king went out with all his household after him. But the king left ten women, concubines, to keep the house. And the king went out with all the people after him, and stopped at the outskirts. Then all his servants passed before him; and all the Cherethites, all the Pelethites, and all the Gittites, six hundred men who had followed him from Gath, passed before the king.

a. **Arise, and let us flee; or we shall not escape from Absalom**: David knew well that Absalom was a ruthless man who valued power over principle. He didn't want the city of Jerusalem to become a battleground (**strike the city with the edge of the sword**), so he fled the city.

b. **The king's... the king... the king**: The writer here wanted to emphasize that *David* was **the king**, despite Absalom's treachery.

c. **The king left ten women, concubines, to keep the house**: David thought - and had reason to think - that these **ten woman** could be safely left behind. He felt he needed someone to look after the house.

i. Sadly, this also tells us that David had at least ten **concubines**. A concubine was essentially a legal mistress. In addition to David's many wives, this shows that David was a man who sometimes indulged his passions instead of restraining them in a godly way.

d. **All the Cherethites, all the Pelethites**: These men comprised David's personal bodyguard. **The Gittites** faithfully followed him from the time he lived among the Philistines (**who followed him from Gath**). These men who were faithful to David *before* he became successful also stuck with him when his success seemed to fade away.

i. It is remarkable that in this defining moment of his latter reign, *foreigners* rallied around David. It is more remarkable - and tragic - that his own countrymen and his own family were nowhere to be found.

e. **Passed before the king**: As David watched this procession leave Jerusalem and head for safety, he was greatly pained. This was reflected in the Psalm that David wrote during this time.

i. David was afraid: *My heart is severely pained within me, and the terrors of death have fallen upon me. Fearfulness and trembling have come upon me, and horror has overwhelmed me. And I said, "Oh that I had wings like a dove! For then I would fly away and be at rest. Indeed, I would wander far off, and remain in the wilderness. I would hasten my escape from the windy storm and tempest."* (Psalm 55:4-8)

ii. David put his trust in God: *LORD, how they have increased who trouble me! Many are they who rise up against me. Many are they who say of me, "There is no help for him in God." But You, O LORD, are a shield for me, my glory and the One who lifts up my head. I cried to the LORD with my voice, and He heard me from His holy hill. I lay down and slept; I awoke, for the LORD sustained me. I will not be afraid of ten thousands of people who have set themselves against me all around.* (Psalm 3:1-6)

iii. Psalms 41, 61, 62, and 63 were also written during this period.

2. (19-23) David's faithful friends.

Then the king said to Ittai the Gittite, "Why are you also going with us? Return and remain with the king. For you *are* a foreigner and also an exile from your own place. In fact, you came *only* yesterday. Should I make you wander up and down with us today, since I go I know not where? Return, and take your brethren back. Mercy and truth *be* with you." And Ittai answered the king and said, *"As* the Lord lives, and *as* my lord the king lives, surely in whatever place my lord the king shall be, whether in death or life, even there also your servant will be." So David said to Ittai, "Go, and cross over." Then Ittai the Gittite and all his men and all the little ones who *were* with him crossed over. And all the country wept with a loud voice, and all the people crossed over. The king himself also crossed over the Brook Kidron, and all the people crossed over toward the way of the wilderness.

a. **Why are you also going with us**: As David watched the procession of his faithful supporters, **Ittai the Gittite** caught his eye. David couldn't understand why this newly arrived foreigner took the risk of such open loyalty to David.

b. **Return and remain with the king**: In calling Absalom **the king**, David showed that he would not cling to the throne. At that moment it seemed that Absalom would succeed, so David called him **the king** and left it unto the Lord.

c. **As my lord the king lives**: Ittai meant *David*, not *Absalom*. David told Ittai, "Remain with the king." Ittai answered back, "That's exactly what I intend to do - and you *are* the king."

d. **Whatever place my lord the king shall be, whether in death or life, even there also your servant will be**: Ittai was loyal to David when it looked certain that it would *cost* him something. True loyalty isn't demonstrated until it is likely to *cost* something to be loyal.

i. "Remember, the more rebels there are, the more need for us to be conspicuously loyal to our King." (Maclaren)

ii. We learn a lot from Ittai's demonstration of loyalty.

- Ittai did it when David was down.
- Ittai did it decisively.
- Ittai did it voluntarily.
- Ittai did it having newly come to David.
- Ittai did it publicly.
- Ittai did it knowing that the fate of David became his fate.

iii. "If Ittai, charmed with David's person and character, though a foreigner and a stranger, felt that he could enlist beneath his banner for life - yea, and declared that he would do so there and then-how much more may you and I, if we know what Christ has done for us, and who He is and what He deserves at our hands, at this good hour plight our troth to Him and vow, 'As the Lord liveth, surely in whatsoever place my Lord and Savior shall be, whether in death or life, even there also shall His servant be.'" (Spurgeon)

iv. We must determine that wherever Jesus is, we will be also. He lives in the heavenlies, so will we be. He is with His church, so will we be. He is busy in His work, so will we be. He is with children, so will we be.

e. **Toward the way of the wilderness**: Many years before, David left the safety of Saul's palace to live as a fugitive. Those years in the wilderness prepared David to be king. God sent David out into **the wilderness** to continue the same work in his life.

i. "Ah! We do not like going over Kedron. When it comes to the pinch, how we struggle against suffering, and especially against dishonor and slander! How many there were who would have gone on pilgrimage, but that Mr. Shame proved too much for them; they could not bear to go over the black brook Kedron, could not endure to be made nothing of for the sake of the Lord of glory, but they even turned back." (Spurgeon)

3. (24-26) David's submission to God's chastening.

There was Zadok also, and all the Levites with him, bearing the ark of the covenant of God. And they set down the ark of God, and Abiathar went up until all the people had finished crossing over from the city. Then the king said to Zadok, "Carry the ark of God back into the city. If I find favor in the eyes of the LORD, He will bring me back and show me *both* it and His dwelling place. But if He says thus: 'I have no delight in you,' here I am, let Him do to me as seems good to Him."

a. **Zadok also, and all the Levites with him, bearing the ark of the covenant of God**: The priests were loyal to David, even though it probably meant death for them if Absalom succeeded. It was good that the men who should be spiritually sensitive to Absalom's evil and David's good were indeed sensitive to it.

b. **Carry the ark of God back into the city**: David trusted in God, not in the ark of the covenant. He was willing to let the ark go back to Jerusalem and to put his fate in God's hands.

c. **If I find favor in the eyes of the Lord, He will bring me back... if He says thus: "I have no delight in you," here I am, let Him do to me as seems good to Him**: David's humble and chastened spirit proved he knew God dealt with him righteously. David submitted to God with an active submission, not a passive one.

4. (27-29) David sends the priests back to gather information.

The king also said to Zadok the priest, *"Are* you *not* a seer? Return to the city in peace, and your two sons with you, Ahimaaz your son, and Jonathan the son of Abiathar. See, I will wait in the plains of the wilderness until word comes from you to inform me." Therefore Zadok and Abiathar carried the ark of God back to Jerusalem. And they remained there.

a. **Are you not a seer**: David recognized that Zadok was a prophet. A man of supernatural insight might be a valuable information source for David.

5. (30) David on the Mount of Olives.

So David went up by the Ascent of the *Mount of* Olives, and wept as he went up; and he had his head covered and went barefoot. And all the people who *were* with him covered their heads and went up, weeping as they went up.

a. **David went up the Ascent of the Mount of Olives**: When Jesus went from the Last Supper to the Garden of Gethsemane to pray, He essentially traced these same steps of David. Both David and Jesus suffered for sin, but Jesus suffered for *our* sins and David suffered for his own.

b. **Wept as he went up; and he had his head covered and went barefoot**: These were emblems of mourning. David was struck by the greatness of this tragedy for the nation, for his family, and for himself.

i. This wasn't a pity-party or soreness merely over the *consequences* of his sin. "He is crushed by the consciousness that his punishment is deserved - the bitter fruit of the sin that filled all his later life with darkness. His courage and his buoyancy have left him." (Maclaren)

ii. "In light of all the facts it is almost certain that the tears David shed as he climbed Olivet, were rather those of humiliation and penitence, than those of self-centered regret. For Absalom there was no excuse, but David carried in his own heart ceaselessly the sense of his own past sin." (Morgan)

iii. This shows David was a redeemed man. Some would say that God let David off easy - that he deserved the death penalty for adultery and murder. If God forgave him and spared David that penalty, surely David would just do it again. Those who think this way do not understand how grace and forgiveness work in the heart of the redeemed. David's sin was ever before him - and in a strange combination of deep gratitude and horror over his forgiven sin, David never did it again.

6. (31-37) David hears of Ahithophel's defection to Absalom.

Then *someone* told David, saying, "Ahithophel *is* among the conspirators with Absalom." And David said, "O LORD, I pray, turn the counsel of Ahithophel into foolishness!" Now it happened when David had come to the top *of the mountain,* where he worshiped God—there was Hushai the Archite coming to meet him with his robe torn and dust on his head. David said to him, "If you go on with me, then you will become a burden to me. But if you return to the city, and say to Absalom, 'I will be your servant, O king; *as I* was your father's servant previously, so I *will* now also *be* your servant,' then you may defeat the counsel of Ahithophel for me. And *do* you not *have* Zadok and Abiathar the priests with you there? Therefore it will be *that* whatever you hear from the king's house, you shall tell to Zadok and Abiathar the priests. Indeed *they have* there with them their two sons, Ahimaaz, Zadok's *son,* and Jonathan, Abiathar's *son;* and by them you shall send me everything you hear." So Hushai, David's friend, went into the city. And Absalom came into Jerusalem.

a. **Turn the counsel of Ahithophel into foolishness**: David knew that Ahithophel was normally a good advisor, but he prayed that he would give foolish counsel to Absalom.

   i. "This was done accordingly: great is the power of faithful prayer. The queen-mother of Scotland was heard to say, that she more feared the prayers of John Knox than an army of fighting men." (Trapp)

b. **David had come to the top of the mountain, where he worshipped God**: David's life was in danger and he had to flee. Yet he took time to stop at the top of the Mount of Olives, look back upon Jerusalem and the tabernacle, and **he worshipped God**. David knew worship was always important and he could worship when circumstances were bad.

b. **Then you may defeat the counsel of Ahithophel for me**: David sent his other aide Hushai back to Jerusalem to frustrate Ahithophel's counsel to Absalom.

c. **Absalom came into Jerusalem**: Absalom came into Jerusalem as a cunning, wicked rebel. David came into Jerusalem as a brave, noble conqueror (2 Samuel 5:6-7). Jesus came into Jerusalem as a servant-king (Matthew 21:4-10).

2 Samuel 16 - David Flees as Absalom Asserts His Reign

A. Ziba's deception.

1. (1-2) Ziba meets David with supplies.

When David was a little past the top *of the mountain,* there was Ziba the servant of Mephibosheth, who met him with a couple of saddled donkeys, and on them two hundred *loaves* of bread, one hundred clusters of raisins, one hundred summer fruits, and a skin of wine. And the king said to Ziba, "What do you mean to do with these?" So Ziba said, "The donkeys *are* for the king's household to ride on, the bread and summer fruit for the young men to eat, and the wine for those who are faint in the wilderness to drink."

a. **Ziba the servant of Mephibosheth**: This Ziba was the servant of Mephibosheth, the son of Jonathan to whom David showed great kindness to (2 Samuel 9).

b. **Who met him with a couple of saddled donkeys**: At a time of great need, Ziba met David with essential supplies. This was a generous and helpful gift from Ziba.

2. (3-4) Ziba speaks against Mephibosheth.

Then the king said, "And where *is* your master's son?" And Ziba said to the king, "Indeed he is staying in Jerusalem, for he said, 'Today the house of Israel will restore the kingdom of my father to me.'" So the king said to Ziba, "Here, all that *belongs* to Mephibosheth *is* yours." And Ziba said, "I humbly bow before you, *that* I may find favor in your sight, my lord, O king!"

a. **He is in Jerusalem**: Ziba told David that Mephibosheth was in Jerusalem, waiting to come to power after David and Absalom ruined each other. Ziba told David that Mephibosheth longed to restore the family of

Saul to power. (**Today the house of Israel will restore the kingdom of my father to me.**)

i. These were lies that Ziba told David and this will be revealed in 2 Samuel 19:24-30. Actually Ziba left Mephibosheth behind to make it *look* as if Mephibosheth did not support David.

ii. This report from Ziba hurt David, because in this time of crisis the last thing he needed to hear was that *another* friend had turned against him. Ziba "was utterly despicable, and the more so because at the moment the sorrow he brought to the heart of David was his feeling that his kindness toward Mephibosheth was ill requited." (Morgan)

iii. This was a "shameless and senseless slander, uttered by a false and faithless sycophant." (Trapp)

b. **All that belongs to Mephibosheth is yours**: David - acting on the only information he had - assumed that Ziba told the truth. Therefore, he rewarded Ziba's loyalty and punished Mephibosheth's reported disloyalty.

i. This was exactly the response Ziba wanted. Ziba was an example of someone who wickedly used a crisis for his own benefit.

B. Shimei curses David.

1. (5-8) Shimei curses a deposed king.

Now when King David came to Bahurim, there was a man from the family of the house of Saul, whose name *was* Shimei the son of Gera, coming from there. He came out, cursing continuously as he came. And he threw stones at David and at all the servants of King David. And all the people and all the mighty men *were* on his right hand and on his left. Also Shimei said thus when he cursed: "Come out! Come out! You bloodthirsty man, you rogue! The Lord has brought upon you all the blood of the house of Saul, in whose place you have reigned; and the Lord has delivered the kingdom into the hand of Absalom your son. So now you *are caught* in your own evil, because you are a bloodthirsty man!"

a. **A man from the family of the house of Saul**: Shimei was a distant relative of the former King Saul, and he still resented David for replacing the dynasty of Saul.

b. **Cursing continuously... threw stones... "You bloodthirsty man, you rogue"**: Shimei was about as offensive as a person could be. He wanted to destroy any shred of dignity or confidence that David had left.

i. There are always people ready to rejoice when a leader falls. Shimei had this heart against David for a long time, but he could only show it when David was down and out.

ii. "It is very hard to bear a cowardly attack. One is very apt to reply and use hard words to one who takes advantage of your position and deals you the coward's blow. Only the coward strikes a man when he is down." (Spurgeon)

c. **The LORD has brought upon you all the blood of the house of Saul... you are caught in your own evil**: A quick look at the outward appearance of things seemed to confirm Shimei's analysis, but Shimei was wrong. None of this came upon David because of what he did to Saul or Saul's family.

i. Shimei was wrong because David actually treated Saul and his family with great love and graciousness.

ii. Shimei was wrong because David was not a bloodthirsty man. It is true that he was a man of war, but not a bloodthirsty man.

iii. Shimei was wrong because David did not bring Saul and his family to ruin - Saul himself brought the family to ruin.

iv. Shimei was *right* that the LORD had brought this upon David, but not for any of the reasons Shimei thought.

2. (9-14) David receives adversity with humility.

Then Abishai the son of Zeruiah said to the king, "Why should this dead dog curse my lord the king? Please, let me go over and take off his head!" But the king said, "What have I to do with you, you sons of Zeruiah? So let him curse, because the LORD has said to him, 'Curse David.' Who then shall say, 'Why have you done so?'" And David said to Abishai and all his servants, "See how my son who came from my own body seeks my life. How much more now *may this* Benjamite? Let him alone, and let him curse; for so the LORD has ordered him. It may be that the LORD will look on my affliction, and that the LORD will repay me with good for his cursing this day." And as David and his men went along the road, Shimei went along the hillside opposite him and cursed as he went, threw stones at him and kicked up dust. Now the king and all the people who *were* with him became weary; so they refreshed themselves there.

a. **Let me go over and take off his head**: Abishai didn't want to listen to Shimei curse or to dodge his stones any more. The mighty men surrounding David were more than ready to kill Shimei in an instant.

b. **So let him curse**: David didn't try to shut up Shimei. He didn't close his ears to unpleasant or critical words. David was willing to hear what God might say to him through a cursing critic.

i. David let Shimei speak because he was not a bloodthirsty man (**what have I to do with you**). Ironically, if David were the kind of man Shimei said he was, Shimei would be dead.

ii. David let Shimei speak because he saw the hand of God in every circumstance (**the LORD has said to him**). He knew that God was more than able to shut Shimei up; David didn't need to give the order.

iii. David let Shimei speak because he put the "Shimei problem" in perspective. (**See how my son who came from my own body seeks my life. How much more now may this Benjamite?**) David knew that his real problem was Absalom not Shimei, and he did not lose this perspective.

iv. David let Shimei speak because he knew that God's hand was on the future as well as the present. (**It may be that the LORD will look on my affliction, and that the LORD will repay me with good for his cursing this day**) David knew that if he did what was right in the present moment, God would take care of the future.

c. **Let him alone, and let him curse**: "David could take this fellow's head off and that in a moment, and yet he said, 'Let him alone. Let him curse.' And this makes a splendid example. If *you can revenge yourself*, DON'T. If you could do it as easily as open your hand, keep it shut. If one bitter word could end the argument, ask for grace to spare that bitter word." (Spurgeon)

d. **So they refreshed themselves there**: David was not without hope or comfort. God allowed comfort to find him, even if it was in the small things. David was able to *receive* the comfort because he was at peace and he knew that God was in control of Israel.

i. In refusing to cling to the throne, David was like Jesus, *who, being in the form of God, did not consider it robbery to be equal with God, but made Himself of no reputation, taking the form of a bondservant, and coming in the likeness of men. And being found in appearance as a man, He humbled Himself and became obedient to the point of death, even the death of the cross* (Philippians 2:6-8). "As we thus follow David through these days of humiliation and shame... we nevertheless understand more perfectly that he was indeed a man after God's own heart." (Morgan)

ii. In his book *A Tale of Three Kings*, Gene Edwards put these words into the mouth of David: "The throne is not mine. Not to have, not to take, not to protect, and not to keep. The throne is the LORD's." It was that kind of heart that kept David on-track through such a difficult time and enabled him to even be **refreshed**.

iii. "This is radiant illustration of the deep and inward peace given to any man who is living in fellowship with God in motive and desire." (Morgan)

C. Absalom's counselors.

1. (15-19) Absalom receives Hushai as an advisor.

Meanwhile Absalom and all the people, the men of Israel, came to Jerusalem; and Ahithophel *was* with him. And so it was, when Hushai the Archite, David's friend, came to Absalom, that Hushai said to Absalom, "*Long* live the king! *Long* live the king!" So Absalom said to Hushai, "*Is* this your loyalty to your friend? Why did you not go with your friend?" And Hushai said to Absalom, "No, but whom the LORD and this people and all the men of Israel choose, his I will be, and with him I will remain. Furthermore, whom should I serve? *Should I not serve* in the presence of his son? As I have served in your father's presence, so will I be in your presence."

a. **When Hushai the Archite, David's friend, came to Absalom**: Hushai wanted to leave with David and support him (2 Samuel 15:32-34). David thought it was better to send Hushai back to Absalom, to both spy on Absalom and to give him bad advice.

i. The bad advice from Hushai was thought necessary because **Ahithophel was with** Absalom. Ahithophel was famous for his wise counsel, and David wanted someone on the inside of Absalom's leadership who might frustrate Ahithophel's counsel.

b. **As I have served in your father's presence, so will I be in your presence**: Hushai lied to Absalom, concealing his motives - like any good spy hides his or her true intentions.

2. (20-23) Absalom follows Ahithophel's advice.

Then Absalom said to Ahithophel, "Give counsel as to what we should do." And Ahithophel said to Absalom, "Go in to your father's concubines, whom he has left to keep the house; and all Israel will hear that you are abhorred by your father. Then the hands of all who are with you will be strong." So they pitched a tent for Absalom on the top of the house, and Absalom went in to his father's concubines in the sight of all Israel. Now the advice of Ahithophel, which he gave in those days,

was as if one had inquired at the oracle of God. So *was* all the advice of Ahithophel both with David and with Absalom.

a. **Ahithophel said to Absalom, "Go into your father's concubines"**: Ahithophel told Absalom to do something so offensive that it would eliminate any possibility of reconciliation with David. Ahithophel felt this strong statement would give courage to Absalom's followers.

> i. In the ancient world, taking the king's concubines was not only an act of immorality; but also, an act of treason. This was a way for Absalom to not only *replace* David but also to completely *repudiate* his father.

> ii. Why did Ahithophel give such radical advice? Because it made sense from his own self-interest. Ahithophel had the most to lose if Absalom failed to keep the throne or if David and Absalom reconciled. He would be revealed and rejected as a traitor.

> iii. The Puritan commentator John Trapp wrote this of Ahithophel's tongue, which gave this wicked advice: "O tongue worthy to have been cut out, shred in gobbets and driven down the throat of him that thus misused him, to the engaging of Absalom in such an unpardonable villainy, beside hazard of his immortal soul!"

b. **So they pitched a tent for Absalom on the top of the house, and Absalom went in to his father's concubines**: This disgraceful act said a lot about *Absalom*, who actually did it. It also said a lot about *Ahithophel*, who must have had a strange sense of satisfaction in seeing David's women violated in a similar way to how his granddaughter Bathsheba was violated.

> i. 2 Samuel 11:3 tells us that Bathsheba's father was **Eliam**, one of David's Mighty Men (2 Samuel 23:34). This also means that her grandfather was Ahithophel (according to 2 Samuel 23:34 and 2 Samuel 15:12).

> ii. This shows the power of bitterness. Ahithophel was willing to see these women abused, Absalom grievously sin, and the kingdom of Israel suffer greatly - all simply to satisfy his bitter longing for revenge.

> iii. This disgraceful incident also shows that God kept His promise to David: *I will take your wives before your eyes and give them to your neighbor, and he shall lie with your wives in the sight of the sun. For you did it secretly, but I will do this thing before all Israel, before the sun* (2 Samuel 12:11-12).

> iv. "Every part of the conduct of Absalom shows him to have been a most profligate young man; he was proud, vindictive, adulterous, incestuous, a parricide, and in fine, reprobate to every good word and work." (Clarke)

c. **Now the advice of Ahithophel, which he gave in those days, was as if one had inquired at the oracle of God**: Ahithophel had a well-deserved reputation for giving counsel almost as good as God. But in this case his counsel was foolish and destructive.

i. It was foolish and destructive because it was motivated by bitterness. Bitterness has the power to turn our best qualities sour.

ii. It was foolish and destructive because God answered David's prayer (2 Samuel 15:31) by prompting Ahithophel to give this foolish counsel, and in prompting Absalom to take the foolish counsel.

iii. Strangely, Absalom thought he could establish his kingdom through immorality. He was a clever and skilled politician but ignorant about the ways of God.

2 Samuel 17 - Absalom Decides His Direction

A. The advice of Ahithophel and of Hushai.

1. (1-4) The counsel of Ahithophel.

Moreover Ahithophel said to Absalom, "Now let me choose twelve thousand men, and I will arise and pursue David tonight. I will come upon him while he *is* weary and weak, and make him afraid. And all the people who *are* with him will flee, and I will strike only the king. Then I will bring back all the people to you. When all return except the man whom you seek, all the people will be at peace." And the saying pleased Absalom and all the elders of Israel.

> a. **I will arise and pursue David tonight**: Ahithophel advised a quick, selective attack against David only (**I will strike only the king**). He advised urgency, doing it all while David was still west of the Jordan River.

> b. **I will strike only the king**: This slip of the tongue was more like an unknowing prophecy. Deep in his heart even Ahithophel knew that David was the real king.

> c. **And the saying please Absalom and all the elders of Israel**: Ahithophel's plan was smart. It was bold and had a high probability of success and it would spare Israel a protracted civil war between the supporters of David and the supporters of Absalom.

2. (5-10) Hushai disagrees with Ahithophel's advice.

Then Absalom said, "Now call Hushai the Archite also, and let us hear what he says too." And when Hushai came to Absalom, Absalom spoke to him, saying, "Ahithophel has spoken in this manner. Shall we do as he says? If not, speak up." So Hushai said to Absalom: "The advice that Ahithophel has given *is* not good at this time." "For," said Hushai, "you know your father and his men, that they *are* mighty men, and they *are* enraged in their minds, like a bear robbed of her cubs in the field; and your father *is* a man of war, and will not camp with the people. Surely

135

by now he is hidden in some pit, or in some *other* place. And it will be, when some of them are overthrown at the first, that whoever hears *it* will say, 'There is a slaughter among the people who follow Absalom.' And even he *who is* valiant, whose heart *is* like the heart of a lion, will melt completely. For all Israel knows that your father *is* a mighty man, and *those* who *are* with him *are* valiant men."

a. **Now call Hushai the Archite**: It is a remarkable evidence of the hand of God and answer to David's prayer in 2 Samuel 15:31 that Absalom even asked for another opinion after such wise, well-received counsel.

b. **The advice that Ahithophel has given is not good at this time**: We can imagine that Hushai's heart sank when heard of the smart plan Ahithophel suggested. He had to quickly think of a counter-plan so that he could defeat the counsel of Ahithophel, as David asked him to do in 2 Samuel 15:32-35.

c. **You know your father and his men, that they are mighty men**: Hushai spoke of the David of the *past*, not the David of the *present*. Hushai saw David with his own eyes and knew that he was not strong and mighty. He hoped that Absalom would vividly remember the David of the past.

d. **Like a bear robbed of her cubs in the field... by now he is hidden is some pit**: Hushai knew David could barely keep himself together, but he effectively painted the picture that David and his men were dangerous and should not be attacked quickly.

e. **There is a slaughter among the people who follow Absalom**: Hushai's point is that it was too risky to attack David immediately. We can imagine that he said all this praying that God would indeed answer David's prayer and defeat the counsel of Ahithophel.

3. (11-13) Hushai advises Absalom to raise a huge army and get David in person.

"Therefore I advise that all Israel be fully gathered to you, from Dan to Beersheba, like the sand that *is* by the sea for multitude, and that you go to battle in person. So we will come upon him in some place where he may be found, and we will fall on him as the dew falls on the ground. And of him and all the men who *are* with him there shall not be left so much as one. Moreover, if he has withdrawn into a city, then all Israel shall bring ropes to that city; and we will pull it into the river, until there is not one small stone found there."

a. **I advise that all Israel be fully gathered**: This would take time. Hushai not only wanted to defeat the counsel of Ahithophel, he also wanted to do whatever he could to buy David more time before the inevitable attack came.

b. **And that you go to battle in person**: This suggestion favored Absalom's vanity. He could prove that *he* was a mighty soldier like his father David. In Ahithophel's plan *Ahithophel* led the battle; in Hushai's plan *Absalom* led the battle.

4. (14) Absalom and the elders favor Hushai's advice.

So Absalom and all the men of Israel said, "The advice of Hushai the Archite *is* better than the advice of Ahithophel." For the LORD had purposed to defeat the good advice of Ahithophel, to the intent that the LORD might bring disaster on Absalom.

a. **The advice of Hushai the Archite is better than the advice of Ahithophel**: This was the first time anyone said *this* - people always favored the advice of Ahithophel. One reason Absalom liked Hushai's advice was because it appealed to his vanity.

b. **The LORD had purposed to defeat the good advice of Ahithophel**: This was the greater reason why the advice of Ahithophel was rejected. God was in control. The throne of Israel belonged to Him, and He could grant it or deny at *His* will.

i. Absalom had the smartest man in Israel on his side, but David's prayer was mightier than Ahithophel's smarts. God led Ahithophel to give foolish counsel that *was* listened to (as in 2 Samuel 16:20-23). God allowed Ahithophel to give great advice and yet have it be rejected. God was in control; **the LORD had purposed**.

ii. "This is one of the great principles of life which every page of the Bible emphasizes and illustrates. Men cannot escape God. They go their own way, but that way never sets them free from the authority and the invincible power of God." (Morgan)

iii. We see that the LORD **purposed to defeat the good advice of Ahithophel** *because David prayed*. Prayer moves the hand of God, and David prayed: *O Lord, I pray, turn the counsel of Ahithophel into foolishness!* (2 Samuel 15:31)

c. **That the LORD might bring disaster on Absalom**: In all of this there was a severe chastening for David, and he knew it. Yet God did not forsake David during this time of chastening. He was there for David at this time also. He was not out to *destroy* David, but to *correct* him.

B. David is warned of Absalom's plan.

1. (15-16) Zadok sends his sons to tell David.

Then Hushai said to Zadok and Abiathar the priests, "Thus and so Ahithophel advised Absalom and the elders of Israel, and thus and so I have advised. Now therefore, send quickly and tell David, saying, 'Do not spend this night in the plains of the wilderness, but speedily cross over, lest the king and all the people who *are* with him be swallowed up.'"

a. **Hushai said to Zadok and Abiathar the priests**: This is exactly what David had in mind when he sent Hushai and the priests back to Absalom (2 Samuel 15:35-36).

b. **Do not spend this night in the plains of the wilderness, but speedily cross over**: Hushai meant that David should **cross over** the Jordan River, giving him room and time to regroup before Absalom's attack.

2. (17-22) David is warned.

Now Jonathan and Ahimaaz stayed at En Rogel, for they dared not be seen coming into the city; so a female servant would come and tell them, and they would go and tell King David. Nevertheless a lad saw them, and told Absalom. But both of them went away quickly and came to a man's house in Bahurim, who had a well in his court; and they went down into it. Then the woman took and spread a covering over the well's mouth, and spread ground grain on it; and the thing was not known. And when Absalom's servants came to the woman at the house, they said, "Where *are* Ahimaaz and Jonathan?" So the woman said to them, "They have gone over the water brook." And when they had searched and could not find *them,* they returned to Jerusalem. Now it came to pass, after they had departed, that they came up out of the well and went and told King David, and said to David, "Arise and cross over the water quickly. For thus has Ahithophel advised against you." So David and all the people who *were* with him arose and crossed over the Jordan. By morning light not one of them was left who had not gone over the Jordan.

a. **A man's house in Bahurim**: Jonathan and Ahimaaz could find help along the way. The whole nation had not gone over to Absalom, especially since he publicly disgraced David's concubines.

b. **So David and all the people who were with him arose and crossed over the Jordan**: Because of this successful intelligence operation, David escaped the immediate danger from Absalom.

3. (23) Ahithophel commits suicide.

Now when Ahithophel saw that his advice was not followed, he saddled a donkey, and arose and went home to his house, to his city. Then he

put his household in order, and hanged himself, and died; and he was buried in his father's tomb.

a. **When Ahithophel saw that his advice was not followed**: Ahithophel did not kill himself over hurt feelings because his counsel was rejected. Instead, he was wise enough to know that under Hushai's plan Absalom would fail and Ahithophel would be implicated in the conspiracy. He knew all was lost.

b. **He put his household in order, and hanged himself**: Ahithophel committed suicide, and we know that suicide is a sin because it is self-murder and God commanded *you shall not murder* (Exodus 20:13). Yet suicide should not be regarded as an unforgivable sin. Anyone who does commit suicide has given in to the lies and deceptions of Satan, whose purpose is to kill and destroy (John 10:10).

i. "Suicide is always the ultimate action of cowardice. In the case of Saul, and in many similar cases, it is perfectly natural; but let it never be glorified as heroic. It is the last resort of the man who dare not stand up to life." (Morgan)

ii. "I desire to call your attention to the text on account of its very remarkable character. '*He put his house in order, and hanged himself.*' To put his house in order, showed that he was a prudent man; to hang himself, proved that he was a fool. Herein is a strange mixture of discretion and desperation, mind and madness. Shall a man have wisdom enough to arrange his worldly affairs with care, and yet shall he be so hapless as to take his own life afterwards?" (Spurgeon)

iii. "Thousands set their houses in order, but destroy their souls; they look well to their flocks and their herds, but not to their hearts' best interests. They gather broken shells with continuous industry, but they throw away priceless diamonds. They exercise forethought, prudence, care, everywhere but where they are most required. They save their money, but squander their happiness; they are guardians of their estates, but suicides of their souls." (Spurgeon)

4. (24-26) Absalom crosses the Jordan to pursue David.

Then David went to Mahanaim. And Absalom crossed over the Jordan, he and all the men of Israel with him. And Absalom made Amasa captain of the army instead of Joab. This Amasa *was* the son of a man whose name *was* Jithra, an Israelite, who had gone in to Abigail the daughter of Nahash, sister of Zeruiah, Joab's mother. So Israel and Absalom encamped in the land of Gilead.

a. **Absalom crossed over the Jordan, he and all the men of Israel with him**: Now Absalom was the head of Israel's army. This was good for Absalom's vanity, but bad for success on the battlefield.

i. "Absalom's vanity ensured his ruin." (Morgan)

b. **Absalom made Amasa captain of the army instead of Joab**: Amasa was the son of a niece of David and a cousin of Joab.

5. (27-29) David finds supporters in Gilead.

Now it happened, when David had come to Mahanaim, that Shobi the son of Nahash from Rabbah of the people of Ammon, Machir the son of Ammiel from Lo Debar, and Barzillai the Gileadite from Rogelim, brought beds and basins, earthen vessels and wheat, barley and flour, parched *grain* and beans, lentils and parched *seeds*, honey and curds, sheep and cheese of the herd, for David and the people who *were* with him to eat. For they said, "The people are hungry and weary and thirsty in the wilderness."

a. **Shobi... Machir... Barzillai**: These otherwise obscure men are given special mention because they helped David in a time of great need. Friends in need are friends indeed.

b. **The people are hungry and weary and thirst in the wilderness**: These helpers of David were not dramatic warriors, but they helped David in this crisis as much as the bravest soldier. They were specially sent by God to comfort David in his affliction.

i. "It was as though God stooped over that stricken soul, and as the blows of the rod cut long furrows in the sufferer's back, the balm of Gliead was poured into the gaping wounds. Voices spoke more gently; hands touched his more softly; pitiful compassion rained tender assurances about his path; and, better than all, the bright-harnessed angels of God's protection encamped about his path and his lying down." (Meyer)

2 Samuel 18 - The Defeat of Absalom

A. Absalom's defeat and death.

1. (1-4) David puts the army under three captains.

And David numbered the people who *were* **with him, and set captains of thousands and captains of hundreds over them. Then David sent out one third of the people under the hand of Joab, one third under the hand of Abishai the son of Zeruiah, Joab's brother, and one third under the hand of Ittai the Gittite. And the king said to the people, "I also will surely go out with you myself." But the people answered, "You shall not go out! For if we flee away, they will not care about us; nor if half of us die, will they care about us. But** *you are* **worth ten thousand of us now. For you are now more help to us in the city." Then the king said to them, "Whatever seems best to you I will do." So the king stood beside the gate, and all the people went out by hundreds and by thousands.**

a. **David numbered the people who were with him, and set captains**: David knew just what to do in organizing his army. He set them into three divisions under the leadership of Joab, Abishai and Ittai the Gittite.

b. **I also will surely go out with you**: David knew that the commander belonged out in the battle. He didn't want to repeat his previous mistake of not going to battle when he should have (2 Samuel 11:1).

c. **You shall not go out**: The people surrounding David would not allow him to go out to battle with the rest of his army. There were three reasons why they insisted on this:

- His life was more valuable (**you are worth ten thousand of us**).

- He could bring reserves if needed (**you are now more help to us in the city**).

- They understood that it would be hard for David to fight against his own son Absalom.

d. **Whatever seems best to you I will do**: David was not stubborn. He knew how to submit to the good advice of others. He did not give up leadership; he practiced good leadership by listening to the wise advice of the people around him.

e. **So the king stood beside the gate, and all the people went out by hundreds and by thousands**: They were willing to take on sacrifice and danger for the benefit of their king. Their devotion to David is an example of how the believer should be devoted to the King of Kings, Jesus Christ.

2. (5) David's command to the three captains.

Now the king had commanded Joab, Abishai, and Ittai, saying, *"Deal gently for my sake with the young man Absalom."* And all the people heard when the king gave all the captains orders concerning Absalom.

a. **Now the king had commanded**: David wanted it clearly known that Absalom was to be captured alive and should not be mistreated in any way.

b. **All the people heard**: David gave this commandment in the presence of all the people so that the captains would feel greater pressure to do what David commanded.

3. (6-8) Absalom's armies are defeated.

So the people went out into the field of battle against Israel. And the battle was in the woods of Ephraim. The people of Israel were overthrown there before the servants of David, and a great slaughter of twenty thousand took place there that day. For the battle there was scattered over the face of the whole countryside, and the woods devoured more people that day than the sword devoured.

a. **So the people went out into the field of battle against Israel**: Those loyal to David fought **against Israel**, because Israel was not loyal to David. Israel was seduced by Absalom's charisma and power.

b. **The people of Israel were overthrown there before the servants of David**: The experienced leadership of David and his captains was probably the main reason for their overwhelming victory.

i. "David had arranged that the battle should take place in this terrain, where the experience and courage of each individual soldier counted more than sheer numbers." (Baldwin)

c. **The woods devoured more people that day than the sword devoured**: This phrase implies that God fought for David in unusual ways. Soldiers loyal to Absalom seemed to be "swallowed up" by the woods.

i. "Perishing not only by the sword, but among the thick oaks and tangled briers of the wood, which concealed fearful precipices and great caverns, into which the rebels plunged in their wild fright when the rout set in." (Spurgeon)

ii. "It is generally supposed that, when the army was broken, the betook themselves to the wood, fell into pits, swamps, and so forth, and being entangled, were hewn down by David's men; but the *Chaldee, Syriac,* and *Arabic,* state that they were *devoured* by *wild beasts* in the wood." (Clarke)

4. (9-17) Joab kills Absalom.

Then Absalom met the servants of David. Absalom rode on a mule. The mule went under the thick boughs of a great terebinth tree, and his head caught in the terebinth; so he was left hanging between heaven and earth. And the mule which *was* under him went on. Now a certain man saw *it* and told Joab, and said, "I just saw Absalom hanging in a terebinth tree!" So Joab said to the man who told him, "You just saw *him!* And why did you not strike him there to the ground? I would have given you ten *shekels* of silver and a belt." But the man said to Joab, "Though I were to receive a thousand *shekels* of silver in my hand, I would not raise my hand against the king's son. For in our hearing the king commanded you and Abishai and Ittai, saying, 'Beware lest anyone *touch* the young man Absalom!' Otherwise I would have dealt falsely against my own life. For there is nothing hidden from the king, and you yourself would have set yourself against *me.*" Then Joab said, "I cannot linger with you." And he took three spears in his hand and thrust them through Absalom's heart, while he was *still* alive in the midst of the terebinth tree. And ten young men who bore Joab's armor surrounded Absalom, and struck and killed him. So Joab blew the trumpet, and the people returned from pursuing Israel. For Joab held back the people. And they took Absalom and cast him into a large pit in the woods, and laid a very large heap of stones over him. Then all Israel fled, everyone to his tent.

a. **Absalom rode on a mule**: Absalom's vanity put him in this battle, against the wise counsel of Ahithophel (2 Samuel 17:1-14). Absalom didn't seem like a great general, riding **a mule** into battle.

b. **His head caught in the terbinth; so he was left hanging between heaven and earth**: Absalom was noted for his good looks and his luxurious hair (2 Samuel 14:25-26). What was his glory was now his curse - Absalom was literally caught by his own hair in the thick trees of the forest.

i. Adam Clarke is careful to point out that the text does not say that Absalom was caught by his hair - we assume that. It may be that he was caught by his neck. Nevertheless, the image remains of Absalom hanging in the tree: "So he hung between heaven and earth, as rejected of both." (Trapp)

ii. "Absalom's end was beset with terrors. When he was caught in the branches of the oak-tree, he was about to sever his hair with a sword stroke, but suddenly he saw hell yawning beneath him, and he preferred to hang in the tree to throwing himself into the abyss alive. Absalom's crime was, indeed, of a nature to deserve the supreme torture, for which reason he is one of the few Jews who have no portion in the world to come." (Ginzberg, *Legends of the Jews*)

c. **I just saw Absalom hanging in a terebinth tree**: When this was reported to Joab, the general wondered why the man did not immediately kill Absalom. The man replied that he did not do it out of obedience and faithfulness to David.

i. Joab insisted he would give both money and a promotion for the one who killed Absalom (**I would have given you ten shekels of silver and a belt**). Yet the man would not do it out of loyalty to David.

ii. "The military belt was the chief ornament of a soldier, and was highly prized in all ancient nations; it was also a rich present from one chieftain to another." (Clarke)

d. **He took three spears in his hand and thrust them through Absalom's heart**: Joab didn't hesitate to strike Absalom, though he knew David commanded him not to. Joab was convinced that it was in David's best interest and in Israel's best interest to show Absalom justice, not mercy.

i. Absalom only received what he deserved. He was a murderer, a traitor, and a rapist. Joab knew that David was generally indulgent towards his children and would never punish Absalom. "He had seen David's action toward his sons characterized by lack of discipline. In the highest interests of the kingdom his hand was raised to slay Absalom." (Morgan)

ii. We might say that Joab was *correct* but not *right*. He was *correct* in understanding that it was better for David and for Israel that Absalom was dead. He was *not right* in disobeying King David, the God-appointed authority over him. By David's dealings with King Saul, we see that God can deal with those in authority, and we don't need to disobey them unless commanded to by Scripture or a clear conscience.

iii. "Long ago he should have died by the hand of justice; and now all his crimes are visited on him in his last act of rebellion. Yet, in the present circumstances, Joab's act was base and disloyal, and a cowardly murder." (Clarke)

iv. At the same time, there is an ironic twist in that the rebel Absalom had his life taken in a rebellious act by Joab. Absalom got what he deserved and Joab would be held accountable for what he did to Absalom, both by God and eventually by David (1 Kings 2:5-6).

e. **Ten young men who bore Joab's armor surrounded Absalom, and struck and killed him**: Absalom was still not dead after three spears because *heart* is a general reference to the middle of the body instead of the specific internal organ.

i. "As he had defiled his father's ten concubines, so by these ten youngsters he hath that little breath that was left in him beaten out of his body." (Trapp)

f. **They took Absalom and cast him into a large pit in the woods, and laid a very large heap of stones over him**: Joab wanted to make sure that Absalom's body was not memorialized as an inspiration to other followers or future rebels.

g. **All Israel fled, everyone to his tent**: This means Absalom's army was in full retreat. David's forces completely carried the day.

5. (18) Absalom's pillar.

Now Absalom in his lifetime had taken and set up a pillar for himself, which *is* in the King's Valley. For he said, "I have no son to keep my name in remembrance." He called the pillar after his own name. And to this day it is called Absalom's Monument.

a. **Absalom in his lifetime had taken and set up a pillar for himself**: This is what we would expect from a self-centered, self-promoting man like Absalom. Joab made sure that Absalom did not have a memorial in death, but Absalom made himself a memorial in life.

b. **I have no son to keep my name in remembrance**: Absalom did have three sons (2 Samuel 14:27). From this statement we surmise that they died before their father did.

B. David hears of Absalom's death.

1. (19-27) Two runners are sent to tell David the outcome of the battle.

Then Ahimaaz the son of Zadok said, "Let me run now and take the news to the king, how the LORD has avenged him of his enemies." And Joab said to him, "You shall not take the news this day, for you shall take the news another day. But today you shall take no news, because the king's son is dead." Then Joab said to the Cushite, "Go, tell the king what you have seen." So the Cushite bowed himself to Joab and ran. And Ahimaaz the son of Zadok said again to Joab, "But whatever happens,

please let me also run after the Cushite." So Joab said, "Why will you run, my son, since you have no news ready?" "But whatever happens," *he said,* "let me run." So he said to him, "Run." Then Ahimaaz ran by way of the plain, and outran the Cushite. Now David was sitting between the two gates. And the watchman went up to the roof over the gate, to the wall, lifted his eyes and looked, and there was a man, running alone. Then the watchman cried out and told the king. And the king said, "If he *is* alone, *there is* news in his mouth." And he came rapidly and drew near. Then the watchman saw *another* man running, and the watchman called to the gatekeeper and said, "There is *another* man, running alone!" And the king said, "He also brings news." So the watchman said, "I think the running of the first is like the running of Ahimaaz the son of Zadok." And the king said, "He *is* a good man, and comes with good news."

> a. **You shall not take the news this day**: Ahimaaz wanted to take David the news of Israel's victory and Absalom's death. But Joab wanted to spare Ahimaaz the son of Zadok the burden of being the messenger of bad news.

> b. **Ahimaaz ran by way of the plain, and outran the Cushite**: Ahimaaz was faster than the other runner. Since the messenger was someone David knew (**Ahimaaz**), he assumed it was good news (**He is a good man, and comes with good news**).

2. (28-32) David learns of Absalom's death from the Cushite, who arrives after Ahimaaz.

And Ahimaaz called out and said to the king, "All is well!" Then he bowed down with his face to the earth before the king, and said, "Blessed *be* the LORD your God, who has delivered up the men who raised their hand against my lord the king!" The king said, "Is the young man Absalom safe?" Ahimaaz answered, "When Joab sent the king's servant and *me* your servant, I saw a great tumult, but I did not know what *it was about*." And the king said, "Turn aside *and* stand here." So he turned aside and stood still. Just then the Cushite came, and the Cushite said, "There is good news, my lord the king! For the LORD has avenged you this day of all those who rose against you." And the king said to the Cushite, "Is the young man Absalom safe?" So the Cushite answered, "May the enemies of my lord the king, and all who rise against you to do harm, be like *that* young man!"

> a. **Is the young man Absalom safe**: This was David's only concern. He should have been more concerned for Israel as a nation than for his traitor son. At the same time, David's question is an example of the great bond

of love between parent and child, and between God our Father and His children.

i. "He might have said, 'Is the young man Absalom dead? For if he is out of the way there will be peace to my realm, and rest to my troubled life.' But no, he is a father, and he must love his own offspring. It is a father that speaks, and a father's love can survive the enmity of a son." (Spurgeon)

ii. "Our children may plunge into the worst of sins, but they are our children still. They may scoff at our God; they may tear our heart to pieces with their wickedness; we cannot take complacency in them, but at the same time we cannot unchild them, nor erase their image from our hearts." (Spurgeon)

b. **I saw a great tumult, but I did not know what it was about**: Compared to the Cushite, Ahimaaz was a better runner but a worse messenger because he didn't know his message. A message can be delivered beautifully, but the messenger's first responsibility is to get the message correct.

c. **May the enemies of my lord the king, and all who rise against you to do harm, be like that young man**: Without saying it directly, the Cushite told David that Absalom was dead.

3. (33) David's great mourning.

Then the king was deeply moved, and went up to the chamber over the gate, and wept. And as he went, he said thus: "O my son Absalom—my son, my son Absalom—if only I had died in your place! O Absalom my son, my son!"

a. **The king was deeply moved**: The Hebrew idea of **deeply moved** implies a violent trembling of the body. David felt completely undone at hearing the news of Absalom's death.

i. In part, David was so **deeply moved** because he knew that he supplied the soil this tragedy grew from.

- The soil came from David's indulgent parenting.
- The soil came from David's sin with Bathsheba and murder of Uriah, after which God promised David: *The sword shall never depart from your house, because you have despised Me, and have taken the wife of Uriah the Hittite to be your wife... I will raise up adversity against you from your own house* (2 Samuel 12:10-11).
- The soil came from David's own sinful indulgence of his passions and smaller rebellions against God, which sins and weaknesses were magnified in his sons.

ii. David's sorrow shows us that it isn't enough that parents train their children to be godly; they must first train *themselves* in godliness. "We cannot stand in the presence of that suffering without learning the solemn lesions of parental responsibility it has to teach, not merely in training our children, but in that earlier training of ourselves for their sakes." (Morgan)

b. **O my son Absalom; my son, my son Absalom**: David mourned so much for Absalom because he really was *his* **son**. David saw his sins, his weaknesses, his rebellion exaggerated in Absalom.

i. "Everything in the story leads up to, and culminates in, this wail of anguish over his dead boy... Five times he repeated the words, 'my son.'" (Morgan)

ii. "This surely had a deeper note in it than that of the merely half-conscious repetition of words occasioned by personal grief. The father recognized how much he was responsible for the son. It is as though he had said: He is indeed my son, his weaknesses are my weaknesses, his passions are my passions, his sins are my sins." (Morgan)

c. **If only I had died in your place**: David wanted to die in the place of his rebellious son. What David could not do God did by dying in the place of rebellious sinners.

i. "So in the cry of David, we actually hear the cry of God, for His lost children. His desire to restore, His desire to forgive." (Smith)

2 Samuel 19 - The Kingdom Is Restored to David

A. David's mourning and Joab's rebuke.

1. (1-3) The effect of David's grief upon his loyal supporters.

And Joab was told, "Behold, the king is weeping and mourning for Absalom." So the victory that day was *turned* into mourning for all the people. For the people heard it said that day, "The king is grieved for his son." And the people stole back into the city that day, as people who are ashamed steal away when they flee in battle.

a. **The victory that day was turned into mourning for all the people**: This was not good. David's loyal and sacrificing supporters won that day for the glory of God and the good of Israel. Then they felt bad about the victory because David was overcome with excessive **weeping and mourning for Absalom**.

i. There is such a thing as *excessive* mourning - mourning that is basically rooted in unbelief and self indulgence. In 1 Thessalonians 4:13, Paul warned Christians: *I do not want you to be ignorant, brethren, concerning those who have fallen asleep, lest you sorrow as others who have no hope.* Some Christians sorrow at times in death or tragedy like those who have *no hope* in God and this is wrong to do.

ii. "If your dear ones are dead you cannot restore them to life by your unbelief; and if they still survive, it will be a pity to be downcast and unbelieving when there is no occasion for it. 'Your strength is to sit still.' Remember that you are a Christian, and a Christian is expected to be more self-possessed than those who have no God to fly to." (Spurgeon)

b. **The people stole back into the city that day, as people who are ashamed**: David's excessive sorrow made his loyal friends and supporter feel **ashamed** they won a great victory.

2. (4-7) Joab rebukes David.

But the king covered his face, and the king cried out with a loud voice, "O my son Absalom! O Absalom, my son, my son!" Then Joab came into the house to the king, and said, "Today you have disgraced all your servants who today have saved your life, the lives of your sons and daughters, the lives of your wives and the lives of your concubines, in that you love your enemies and hate your friends. For you have declared today that you regard neither princes nor servants; for today I perceive that if Absalom had lived and all of us had died today, then it would have pleased you well. Now therefore, arise, go out and speak comfort to your servants. For I swear by the LORD, if you do not go out, not one will stay with you this night. And that will be worse for you than all the evil that has befallen you from your youth until now."

a. **O my son Absalom! O Absalom, my son, my son**: David could not stop singing this song. He was still locked into his excessive mourning and lack of perspective. He was mastered by his feelings, and feelings were never meant to master us.

i. God is not *against* feelings - not at all. Many Christians lack deep and profound feeling and experience in their walk with God. At the same time, feelings were never meant to master over us.

ii. David's problem was not in what he *knew* - Absalom's tragic death and David's own role in it. David's problem was in what he *forgot* - that God was still in control, that a great victory was won, that he had many loyal supporters, and that God showed great grace and mercy to David. When someone is overcome in tragedy or sorrow, the problem is not in what they *know*, but in what they *forget*.

iii. "Who ever heard David cry out in godly sorrow, O Uriah, would God I had died for thee!" (Trapp)

b. **Today you have disgraced all your servants who today have saved your life**: Joab gave David a stern wake-up call. "David, your excessive mourning is selfish. It isn't all about you. These loyal, sacrificial supporters of yours deserve to feel good about their victory and you are making them feel terrible. Snap out of it."

c. **I perceive that if Absalom had lived and all of us had died today, then it would have pleased you well**: This is a sharp truth delivered with precision. Joab wanted David not only to see that he was *foolish* in his excessive grief, but he was also *selfish*.

d. **Now therefore, arise, go out and speak comfort to your servants**: "Go out and encourage the team - they deserve it. If you don't you will lose most of them."

3. (8) David receives Joab's rebuke.

Then the king arose and sat in the gate. And they told all the people, saying, "There is the king, sitting in the gate." So all the people came before the king. For everyone of Israel had fled to his tent.

a. **Then the king arose and sat in the gate**: David didn't *feel* like doing this. His *feelings* told him to stay locked into his excessive mourning. Yet David let his understanding of what was *right* be bigger than what he *felt*.

i. We never again hear David crying out, "*O Absalom.*" Doing what he needed to do got that song out of his head.

b. **So all the people came before the king**: This is what they needed to see - David sitting as king in the place of authority (**sitting in the gate**). This told them that their sacrifice was worth it, that it was appreciated, and that David would continue to reign. Joab's rebuke worked because Joab cared enough to say it, and David was wise enough to receive it.

B. Israel returns to David.

1. (9-10) The tribes debate receiving David back as king.

Now all the people were in a dispute throughout all the tribes of Israel, saying, "The king saved us from the hand of our enemies, he delivered us from the hand of the Philistines, and now he has fled from the land because of Absalom. But Absalom, whom we anointed over us, has died in battle. Now therefore, why do you say nothing about bringing back the king?"

a. **All the people were in a dispute throughout all the tribes of Israel**: David survived Absalom's attempted overthrow, but the kingdom was not yet restored to David.

b. **The king saved us... But Absalom, whom we anointed over us, has died**: The tribes of Israel understood what David did for them, they understood that they rejected him and embraced Absalom, and they understood that Absalom was now dead. It left the people of Israel **in a dispute** about **bringing back the king**.

i. They only seemed to want David back after the false king Absalom failed. In the same way, we often only decide to bring back King Jesus when our false kings fail.

ii. "The folly of their allegiance to Absalom was clear - it had brought only misery and confusion. They were on the wrong side; they had

rejected their true king, and therefore the situation was full of unrest."
(Redpath)

2. (11-14) David sends negotiators to the tribes.

**So King David sent to Zadok and Abiathar the priests, saying, "Speak
to the elders of Judah, saying, 'Why are you the last to bring the king
back to his house, since the words of all Israel have come to the king,
to his *very* house? You *are* my brethren, you *are* my bone and my flesh.
Why then are you the last to bring back the king?' And say to Amasa,
'*Are* you not my bone and my flesh? God do so to me, and more also,
if you are not commander of the army before me continually in place
of Joab.'" So he swayed the hearts of all the men of Judah, just as *the
heart of* one man, so that they sent *this word* to the king: "Return, you
and all your servants!"**

> a. **Why are you the last to bring the king back to his very house**: David
> would not *force* his reign on Israel. He would only come back if the tribes
> who rejected him for Absalom agreed to **bring back the king**.
>
> > i. "David didn't lift a finger to re-establish his authority... His return to
> > sovereignty was decided by the voluntary submission of his kinsmen
> > and by their loving obedience to his will." (Redpath)
>
> b. **Amasa... commander of the army... in place of Joab**: David agreed to
> replace Joab with Amasa, who was the captain of Absalom's army. This was
> to put Joab in his place and to offer a gesture of reconciliation to the former
> supporters of Absalom.
>
> c. **So he swayed the hearts of all the men of Judah, just as the heart
> of one man**: The efforts of Zadok and Abiathar succeeded. David would
> not come back until welcomed by the **hearts of all**, and that could not be
> *forced* - their hearts had to be **swayed**.
>
> > i. God will not force His reign on us. We must welcome His reign and
> > He will not force our heart response. Our hearts must be **swayed** by
> > the work of the Word of God and the Holy Spirit.
> >
> > ii. **Just as the heart of one man**: David wanted the reception to be
> > *unanimous*. The men of Judah responded together to the wooing work
> > of Zadok and Abiathar.

3. (15-18a) David comes over the Jordan River, helped by Judah and Benjamin.

**Then the king returned and came to the Jordan. And Judah came to
Gilgal, to go to meet the king, to escort the king across the Jordan. And
Shimei the son of Gera, a Benjamite, who *was* from Bahurim, hastened
and came down with the men of Judah to meet King David. *There were***

a thousand men of Benjamin with him, and Ziba the servant of the
house of Saul, and his fifteen sons and his twenty servants with him;
and they went over the Jordan before the king. Then a ferryboat went
across to carry over the king's household, and to do what he thought
good.

a. **Then the king returned**: The point is emphasized - David would not
return as king until he was welcomed, until hearts were swayed to receive
him.

b. **To escort the king**: David left Israel as a desperate fugitive, rejected
by the nation and hunted by his son Absalom. He came back escorted by
thousands of enthusiastic supporters.

C. David's kindness to his subjects.

1. (18b-23) David shows forgiveness to Shimei.

Now Shimei the son of Gera fell down before the king when he had
crossed the Jordan. Then he said to the king, "Do not let my lord impute
iniquity to me, or remember what wrong your servant did on the day
that my lord the king left Jerusalem, that the king should take *it* to
heart. For I, your servant, know that I have sinned. Therefore here I
am, the first to come today of all the house of Joseph to go down to meet
my lord the king." But Abishai the son of Zeruiah answered and said,
"Shall not Shimei be put to death for this, because he cursed the LORD's
anointed?" And David said, "What have I to do with you, you sons of
Zeruiah, that you should be adversaries to me today? Shall any man be
put to death today in Israel? For do I not know that today I *am* king
over Israel?" Therefore the king said to Shimei, "You shall not die."
And the king swore to him.

a. **I, your servant, know that I have sinned**: Shimei showed a remarkably
humble, contrite confession. He sinned greatly against David, and here he
repented greatly before him.

i. Shimei's repentance was humble (**fell down before the king**). His
posture represented his low place before David.

ii. Shimei's repentance honored David (**Do not let my lord impute
iniquity to me**). He knew David had the right to **impute iniquity**,
but he pleaded for mercy.

iii. Shimei's repentance was honest (**I have sinned**). He made no
attempt to minimize his actions.

iv. Shimei's repentance was put into action (**here I am, the first to
come today of all the house of Joseph to go down to meet my lord**

the king). Real repentance will show itself not only in words and ideas, but also in *action*.

b. **The king said to Shimei, "You shall not die"**: David spared the life of Shimei, showing forgiveness to the man who formerly bitterly cursed him (2 Samuel 16:5-13).

> i. "Perhaps you have been like Shimei, who cursed king David, and you are afraid that Jesus will never forgive you. But David forgave Shimei, and Jesus is ready to forgive you. He delighteth in mercy. I do believe that the harps of heaven never give to Christ such happiness as he has when he forgives the ungodly, and saith, 'Thy sins are forgiven; go in peace.'" (Spurgeon)

c. **Do I not know that today I am king over Israel**: David could readily forgive a man who deserved to die because he was *secure*, knowing that *God* gave him the throne. Insecurity is a great motivator for revenge and holding on to bitterness.

2. (24-30) David shows understanding to Mephibosheth.

Now Mephibosheth the son of Saul came down to meet the king. And he had not cared for his feet, nor trimmed his mustache, nor washed his clothes, from the day the king departed until the day he returned in peace. So it was, when he had come to Jerusalem to meet the king, that the king said to him, "Why did you not go with me, Mephibosheth?" And he answered, "My lord, O king, my servant deceived me. For your servant said, 'I will saddle a donkey for myself, that I may ride on it and go to the king,' because your servant *is* lame. And he has slandered your servant to my lord the king, but my lord the king *is* like the angel of God. Therefore do *what is* good in your eyes. For all my father's house were but dead men before my lord the king. Yet you set your servant among those who eat at your own table. Therefore what right have I still to cry out anymore to the king?" So the king said to him, "Why do you speak anymore of your matters? I have said, 'You and Ziba divide the land.'" Then Mephibosheth said to the king, "Rather, let him take it all, inasmuch as my lord the king has come back in peace to his own house."

a. **Mephibosheth the son of Saul came down to meet the king**: Mephibosheth was the son of Jonathan and the last surviving heir to the dynasty of Saul. 2 Samuel 9 told how David showed unique kindness to Mephibosheth. 2 Samuel 16:1-4 described how Ziba, the servant of Mephibosheth, met David with supplies as he left Jerusalem. Ziba said that Mephibosheth abandoned David and hoped to gain from the conflict between David and Absalom.

b. **My lord, O king, my servant deceived me**: Mephibosheth explained why he did not join David, and how Ziba **slandered** him before David.

c. **You set your servant among those who eat at your own table. Therefore what right have I still to cry out anymore to the king**: Though Mephibosheth was slandered before David, Mephibosheth didn't defend himself or demand a hearing before David. He knew David already gave him more than he deserved, so if David were to now take it all away he would still be ahead.

d. **You and Ziba divide the land**: When Ziba told David that Mephibosheth abandoned him, David granted Ziba all of Mephibosheth's land and property (2 Samuel 16:4). Hearing the whole story, David didn't go back on his promise to Ziba even though it was made under fraudulent circumstances. Yet he did lessen Ziba's reward by offering a split between Ziba and Mephibosheth of all the property from Saul's house.

e. **Rather, let him take it all, inasmuch as my lord the king has come back in peace to his own house**: Mephibosheth was content to let Ziba have all the property if he could only know that David reigned. David's reign was more important to him than his personal enrichment.

i. "For his own enrichment this man cared nothing at all. It was everything to him that his king should come into the possession of his kingdom in peace... It is to be feared that too often we are more concerned about our rights than about His. It is a great and glorious thing when our loyalty and love make us far more concerned about the victories of our Lord, than about our own unquestioned rights. Yet that should be the normal attitude of all who sit at the King's Table." (Morgan)

3. (31-39) David shows appreciation to Barzillai.

And Barzillai the Gileadite came down from Rogelim and went across the Jordan with the king, to escort him across the Jordan. Now Barzillai was a very aged man, eighty years old. And he had provided the king with supplies while he stayed at Mahanaim, for he *was* a very rich man. And the king said to Barzillai, "Come across with me, and I will provide for you while you are with me in Jerusalem." But Barzillai said to the king, "How long have I to live, that I should go up with the king to Jerusalem? I *am* today eighty years old. Can I discern between the good and bad? Can your servant taste what I eat or what I drink? Can I hear any longer the voice of singing men and singing women? Why then should your servant be a further burden to my lord the king? Your servant will go a little way across the Jordan with the king. And why should the king repay me *with* such a reward? Please let your servant

turn back again, that I may die in my own city, near the grave of my father and mother. But here is your servant Chimham; let him cross over with my lord the king, and do for him what seems good to you." And the king answered, "Chimham shall cross over with me, and I will do for him what seems good to you. Now whatever you request of me, I will do for you." Then all the people went over the Jordan. And when the king had crossed over, the king kissed Barzillai and blessed him, and he returned to his own place.

a. **Come across with me, and I will provide for you while you are with me in Jerusalem**: Barzillai brought essential help to David when he fled Jerusalem as Absalom took over the city. In gratitude, David offered him the honor of living with the king in Jerusalem.

i. **He was a very rich man**: Barzillai was a man of great resources - and he wisely used those resources to support the servant of God and the cause of God. In Luke 12:21, Jesus spoke of the foolish man *who lays up treasure for himself, and is not rich toward God.* Barzillai was wise enough to use his resources to lay up treasure in heaven and he *was* rich toward God.

b. **Why should the king repay me with such a reward**: Barzillai did not do this for the sake of reward. He gave out of a right heart, not from the motive of self-exaltation.

c. **Here is your servant Chimham; let him cross over with my lord the king**: Barzillai respectfully declined the honor for himself but accepted it on behalf of his son Chimham.

i. "It is generally understood that this was Barzillai's son; and this is probable from 1 Kings 2:7, where, when David was dying, he said, *Show kindness to the sons of Barzillai.*" (Clarke)

4. (40-43) Israel and Judah quarrel about David.

Now the king went on to Gilgal, and Chimham went on with him. And all the people of Judah escorted the king, and also half the people of Israel. Just then all the men of Israel came to the king, and said to the king, "Why have our brethren, the men of Judah, stolen you away and brought the king, his household, and all David's men with him across the Jordan?" So all the men of Judah answered the men of Israel, "Because the king *is* a close relative of ours. Why then are you angry over this matter? Have we ever eaten at the king's *expense?* Or has he given us any gift?" And the men of Israel answered the men of Judah, and said, "We have ten shares in the king; therefore we also have more *right* to David than you. Why then do you despise us—were we not the

first to advise bringing back our king?" Yet the words of the men of
Judah were fiercer than the words of the men of Israel.

a. **All the people of Judah escorted the king, and also half the people
of Israel**: The northern tribes felt excluded in this ceremonial welcoming
back of David from across the Jordan River.

b. **Why have our brethren, the men of Judah, stolen you away... why
then are you angry... why then do you despise us**: This argument was
ultimately about who was more loyal to King David, and who had the
greater right to honor him.

c. **Why then do you despise us**: The ten northern tribes felt unappreciated
by the tribe of Judah. This competitive attitude between Judah and the ten
northern tribes set the stage for civil war in David's day and the eventual
division of the nation into two.

2 Samuel 20 - The Rebellion of Sheba

A. David returns to Jerusalem and to an insurrection.

1. (1-2) Sheba's rebellion.

And there happened to be there a rebel, whose name *was* Sheba the son of Bichri, a Benjamite. And he blew a trumpet, and said:

"We have no share in David,
Nor do we have inheritance in the son of Jesse;
Every man to his tents, O Israel!"

So every man of Israel deserted David, *and* followed Sheba the son of Bichri. But the men of Judah, from the Jordan as far as Jerusalem, remained loyal to their king.

    a. **There happened to be a rebel**: Sheba took advantage of David's weakened position after Absalom's failed rebellion and the conflict between Judah and the other ten tribes (2 Samuel 19:40-43). He based his rebellion on three principles common to rebels:

- **We have no share in David**: Sheba *denied the king's sovereignty*. He claimed that David had no right to reign over him or the ten tribes of Israel.

- **The son of Jesse**: Sheba *devalued the king's identity*. Jesse was a humble farmer and Sheba wanted to emphasize David's humble beginning.

- **Every man to his tents**: Sheba *decided to go his own way* and drew others with him. He acted on his low opinion of David.

    i. G. Campbell Morgan thought the phrase "**We have no share in David, nor do we have an inheritance in the son of Jesse**" was an effective slogan promoted by Sheba. "The story should teach us that popular and plausible catchwords ought to be received and acted upon with great caution."

b. **Israel deserted David**: Sheba succeeded in drawing away the ten northern tribes and David had another civil war to deal with.

i. In 2 Samuel 19:40-43 leaders from these same ten tribes argued with the tribe of Judah over who honored David more. Their response to Sheba's rebellion shows that their desire to honor David had nothing to do with honoring him, but in exalting self.

ii. We might say that the tribe of Judah treated the other ten tribes unfairly, but "Injustice is never corrected by a yet deeper wrong." (Morgan)

iii. We might say that it is in the nature of men to divide. We have to be held together by the Holy Spirit. Paul put it like this: *I, therefore, the prisoner of the Lord, beseech you to walk worthy of the calling with which you were called, with all lowliness and gentleness, with longsuffering, bearing with one another in love, endeavoring to keep the unity of the Spirit in the bond of peace* (Ephesians 4:1-3). We don't *make* the unity of the Spirit, we *keep* the unity of the Spirit - but we must *keep* what He *makes*.

c. **The men of Judah... remained loyal to their king**: The desertion of the ten tribes was distressing but the loyalty of **the men of Judah** was wonderful. When others desert or divide it gives a greater opportunity to demonstrate loyalty.

i. We should imitate the loyalty Judah showed to their king. This means we must be loyal to Jesus in spite of the mocking of the multitude. We must be loyal to Jesus in spite of the rebellion of the flesh. We must be loyal to Jesus in spite of the times when He seems distant.

2. (3) David puts away the women Absalom violated.

Now David came to his house at Jerusalem. And the king took the ten women, his concubines whom he had left to keep the house, and put them in seclusion and supported them, but did not go in to them. So they were shut up to the day of their death, living in widowhood.

a. **Put them in seclusion**: Absalom raped these ten concubines as part of his rebellion against David (2 Samuel 16:20-23). Upon his return, David set them aside as unfortunate victims of Absalom's sin.

i. "He could not well divorce them; he could not punish them, as they were not in the transgression; he could not more be familiar with them, because they had been defiled by his son; and to have married them to other men might have been dangerous to the state." (Clarke)

b. **They were shut up to the day of their death, living in widowhood**: The sad fate of David's ten concubines is an example of how our sin often has horrible effects on others. They suffered because of Absalom's sin - and David's sin.

3. (4-5) David tells Amasa to marshal an army to deal with Sheba's rebellion.

And the king said to Amasa, "Assemble the men of Judah for me within three days, and be present here yourself." So Amasa went to assemble *the men of* **Judah. But he delayed longer than the set time which David had appointed him.**

a. **The king said to Amasa**: Amasa was Absalom's former general and David made him the commander of his army as a conciliatory move after the death of Absalom.

b. **Assemble the men of Judah for me within three days**: David knew that time was of the essence. When Absalom had the chance to quickly crush David, he did not take advantage of the opportunity. David did not want to make the same mistake with Sheba.

c. **He delayed longer than the set time**: Amasa wasn't up to the job David gave him. He was not a completely competent military man, and Joab (the former commander of David's army) defeated Amasa soundly when they fought together.

4. (6-7) Tired of waiting, David sends his royal guard.

And David said to Abishai, "Now Sheba the son of Bichri will do us more harm than Absalom. Take your lord's servants and pursue him, lest he find for himself fortified cities, and escape us." So Joab's men, with the Cherethites, the Pelethites, and all the mighty men, went out after him. And they went out of Jerusalem to pursue Sheba the son of Bichri.

a. **David said to Abishai**: David gave these orders to Abishai. He was the commander over **your lord's servants** - David's personal guard.

b. **So Joab's men... and all the mighty men, went out**: Joab was the field commander of these troops, but Abishai was in command over him.

B. Joab kills Amasa and defeats Sheba.

1. (8-10) Using deception, Joab murders Amasa.

When they *were* **at the large stone which** *is* **in Gibeon, Amasa came before them. Now Joab was dressed in battle armor; on it was a belt** *with* **a sword fastened in its sheath at his hips; and as he was going forward, it fell out. Then Joab said to Amasa,** *"Are* **you in health, my brother?" And Joab took Amasa by the beard with his right hand to**

kiss him. But Amasa did not notice the sword that *was* in Joab's hand. And he struck him with it in the stomach, and his entrails poured out on the ground; and he did not *strike* him again. Thus he died. Then Joab and Abishai his brother pursued Sheba the son of Bichri.

a. **Amasa came before them**: Amasa didn't assemble the army of Judah quickly enough, but he didn't want to be left out of the battle. He joined the troops loyal to David at **Gibeon**.

b. **Joab took Amasa by the beard**: Joab approached Amasa with cunning and deception. Holding the beard was a sign of a friendly welcome, and the fallen sword made it seem that Joab was unarmed.

c. **He struck him with it in the stomach**: Joab showed how ruthless he was. He murdered Amasa - the man who replaced him as commander of David's armies - out of both rivalry and concern that Amasa did not genuinely support David.

i. "It is very likely that Amasa did not immediately die: I have known instances of persons living several hours after their bowels had been shed out." (Clarke)

2. (11-14) Joab takes command of the troops loyal to David.

Meanwhile one of Joab's men stood near Amasa, and said, "Whoever favors Joab and whoever *is* for David—follow Joab!" But Amasa wallowed in *his* blood in the middle of the highway. And when the man saw that all the people stood still, he moved Amasa from the highway to the field and threw a garment over him, when he saw that everyone who came upon him halted. When he was removed from the highway, all the people went on after Joab to pursue Sheba the son of Bichri. And he went through all the tribes of Israel to Abel and Beth Maachah and all the Berites. So they were gathered together and also went after *Sheba*.

a. **All the people went on after Joab**: For all his ruthless devotion to David, Joab was a true leader. The soldiers naturally followed the commander who successfully led them many times before.

b. **He went through all the tribes of Israel**: Joab was able to find men loyal to David in all the tribes of Israel. Though Sheba was able to assemble an army against David, there were still many people loyal to David.

3. (15-122) The end of Sheba's rebellion.

Then they came and besieged him in Abel of Beth Maachah; and they cast up a siege mound against the city, and it stood by the rampart. And all the people who *were* with Joab battered the wall to throw it down. Then a wise woman cried out from the city, "Hear, Hear! Please say to

Joab, 'Come nearby, that I may speak with you.'" When he had come near to her, the woman said, *"Are* you Joab?" He answered, "I *am."* Then she said to him, "Hear the words of your maidservant." And he answered, "I am listening." So she spoke, saying, "They used to talk in former times, saying, 'They shall surely seek *guidance* at Abel,' and so they would end *disputes.* I *am among the* peaceable *and* faithful in Israel. You seek to destroy a city and a mother in Israel. Why would you swallow up the inheritance of the LORD?" And Joab answered and said, "Far be it, far be it from me, that I should swallow up or destroy! That *is* not so. But a man from the mountains of Ephraim, Sheba the son of Bichri by name, has raised his hand against the king, against David. Deliver him only, and I will depart from the city." So the woman said to Joab, "Watch, his head will be thrown to you over the wall." Then the woman in her wisdom went to all the people. And they cut off the head of Sheba the son of Bichri, and threw *it* out to Joab. Then he blew a trumpet, and they withdrew from the city, every man to his tent. So Joab returned to the king at Jerusalem.

a. **A wise woman cried out from the city**: When Sheba took refuge in the city of Abel, Joab set a siege against the city. Siege warfare was a terrible ordeal for the citizens of the besieged city, and this **wise woman** was smart enough to seek a speedy end to the struggle.

b. **Deliver him only, and I will depart from the city**: Joab was a practical man. He had nothing against the city of Abel, only against Sheba. If the people of Abel helped him get Sheba it was all the better.

c. **They cut off the head of Sheba the son of Bichri, and threw it out to Joab**: Sheba probably thought he was safe within the walls of that city, but no one is safe when they run against God's will. There isn't a wall high enough or strong enough to protect against God and His will.

i. We can make a spiritual analogy out of Sheba, his rebellion, and his refuge in the city of Abel. "Every man's breast is a city enclosed. Every sin is a traitor that lurketh within those walls. God calleth for Sheba's head, neither hath he any quarrel to us for our person, but for our sin. If we love the head of our traitor above the life of our soul, we shall justly perish in the vengeance." (Trapp)

ii. "It were happy if all such traitors might hop headless." (Trapp)

iii. So ended the rebellion of Sheba. Yet the division between Judah and the other eleven tribes of Israel remained. After the death of Solomon there was a civil war that permanently divided the twelve tribes into two nations: the southern Kingdom of Judah and the northern Kingdom of Israel.

4. (23-26) David's second administration.

And Joab *was* over all the army of Israel; Benaiah the son of Jehoiada *was* over the Cherethites and the Pelethites; Adoram *was* in charge of revenue; Jehoshaphat the son of Ahilud *was* recorder; Sheva *was* scribe; Zadok and Abiathar *were* the priests; and Ira the Jairite was a chief minister under David.

a. **Joab was over all the army of Israel**: Though he gained the position through murder, David allowed Joab to take control over the armies of Israel.

b. **Benaiah... Adoram... Jehoshaphat... Sheva... Zadok and Abiathar... Ira the Jairite**: The greatness of David's kingdom was not built on David's abilities alone. He knew how to assemble and lead an effective team.

i. Some think that the idea behind the phrase "**chief minister**" is that Ira was sort of a chaplain to David. "He was probably a sort of *domestic chaplain* to the king." (Clarke)

ii. If David - a man after God's heart and the sweet psalmist of Israel - needed devotional "help," we should not think ourselves above it.

2 Samuel 21 - Avenging the Gibeonites

A. David avenges the Gibeonites.

1. (1) A three-year famine prompts David to seek God.

Now there was a famine in the days of David for three years, year after year; and David inquired of the LORD. And the LORD answered, "It is because of Saul and his bloodthirsty house, because he killed the Gibeonites."

a. **And David inquired of the LORD**: David wisely sought God in the face of chronic problems. David was concerned after the first year of famine, and even more after the second - but two years of famine didn't make him look to a spiritual cause. Yet after three years of famine, **David inquired of the LORD**.

i. David didn't see a spiritual reason in *every* problem, but he did not shut his eyes to the hand of God in circumstances.

ii. "The first and second year he might look upon it as a punishment laid upon them for the common sins of the land: but when he saw it continuing a third year also, he thought there was something in it more than ordinary, and therefore, although he well knew the natural cause to be drought, yet he inquired after the supernatural, as wise men should do." (Trapp)

b. **It is because of Saul and his bloodthirsty house, because he killed the Gibeonites**: This massacre isn't recorded in 1 Samuel, but David didn't question that it happened. Apparently at some time during his reign Saul attacked and killed many of the Gibeonites.

i. "The whole people suffered for Saul's sin; either because they approved it, or at least bewailed it not; neither did what they could to hinder it; whereby they became accessory." (Trapp)

c. **He killed the Gibeonites**: When David heard it was because of an attack against the **Gibeonites**, a chill probably ran up his back. He knew they were a people *especially* wrong for Saul to attack and kill.

i. In the days of Joshua - more than 400 years before David's time - Israel swore not to harm the Gibeonites, a neighboring tribe (Joshua 9). God expected Israel to keep its promise, even though the Gibeonites tricked Israel into making the agreement. Saul's crime was not only in killing the Gibeonites but also in breaking this ancient and important oath.

ii. This emphasizes many important principles:

- God expects us to keep our promises.

- God expects nations to keep their promises.

- Time does not diminish our obligation to promises.

- God's correction may come a long time after the offense.

iii. If God has such a high expectation that men keep their covenants, we can have great confidence that He will keep His covenant with us. There is an emerald rainbow around the throne of God to proclaim His remembrance to His everlasting covenant with His people (Revelation 4:3).

2. (2) David speaks to the Gibeonites.

So the king called the Gibeonites and spoke to them. Now the Gibeonites *were* not of the children of Israel, but of the remnant of the Amorites; the children of Israel had sworn protection to them, but Saul had sought to kill them in his zeal for the children of Israel and Judah.

a. **The king called the Gibeonites**: David knew he had to do something about this and so he initiated a resolution with the Gibeonites.

b. **Saul had sought to kill them in his zeal for the children of Israel and Judah**: We normally think of such zeal as something good. Yet Saul's *misguided* zeal was a sin and brought calamity on Israel.

i. This is a good example of how *good intentions* don't excuse *bad actions*. We often excuse bad actions in ourselves and in others because of what we think are good intentions. But God examines both our *intentions* and our *actions*.

3. (3-6) David's agreement with the Gibeonites.

Therefore David said to the Gibeonites, "What shall I do for you? And with what shall I make atonement, that you may bless the inheritance of the LORD?" And the Gibeonites said to him, "We will have no silver or gold from Saul or from his house, nor shall you kill any man in Israel

for us." So he said, "Whatever you say, I will do for you." Then they answered the king, "As for the man who consumed us and plotted against us, *that* we should be destroyed from remaining in any of the territories of Israel, let seven men of his descendants be delivered to us, and we will hang them before the LORD in Gibeah of Saul, *whom* the LORD chose." And the king said, "I will give *them.*"

a. **What shall I do for you**: In resolving this matter with the Gibeonites, David did not dictate terms to them. He came to them as a servant, not as a king.

b. **That you may bless the inheritance of the LORD**: David felt that if the Gibeonites could **bless** Israel then the reconciliation would be complete, and God's chastening of Israel would end.

c. **We will have no silver or gold from Saul or from his house, nor shall you kill any man in Israel for us**: The Gibeonites made it clear that they didn't want money or direct retribution. Though Saul made a wholesale slaughter of the Gibeonites, they didn't ask for the same among the people of Israel.

d. **Let seven men of his descendants be delivered to us**: In those ancient times the request of the Gibeonites was considered reasonable. Instead of money or an "eye for an eye" they only asked for justice against Saul through his descendants. David agreed to this (**I will give them**).

i. "Which God had now a purpose to root out, that they might not be further troublesome to David - who had lately suffered so much - in the quiet enjoyment of the kingdom." (Trapp)

e. **I will give them**: David knew this was the right thing to do. Some believe he knew it was right because David knew that Saul's descendants helped in or benefited directly from that massacre.

i. Obviously, we are not told *everything* about this incident; we must trust the principle stated by Abraham: *Shall not the Judge of all the earth do right?* (Genesis 18:25)

4. (7-9) David fulfills the agreement with the Gibeonites.

But the king spared Mephibosheth the son of Jonathan, the son of Saul, because of the LORD's oath that *was* between them, between David and Jonathan the son of Saul. So the king took Armoni and Mephibosheth, the two sons of Rizpah the daughter of Aiah, whom she bore to Saul; and the five sons of Michal the daughter of Saul, whom she brought up for Adriel the son of Barzillai the Meholathite; and he delivered them into the hands of the Gibeonites, and they hanged them on the hill before the Lord. So they fell, *all* seven together, and were put to death in the days of harvest, in the first *days,* in the beginning of barley harvest.

a. **The king spared Mephibosheth**: Mephibosheth was the most notable living descendant of Saul and it made the most sense to put him as the first of the seven to be delivered to the Gibeonites for execution. Yet David promised to protect and bless Mephibosheth and he would not fulfill one promise at the expense of another.

b. **They hanged them on the hill before the Lord**: David chose seven male descendants of Saul to give over to the Gibeonites and they executed them by public hanging. The phrase **before the Lord** implies God approved of their execution.

i. The *method* of death was also important because it fulfilled the promise of Deuteronomy 21:23: *he who is hanged is accursed of God.* These descendants of Saul bore the curse Saul deserved and so delivered Israel from the guilt of their sin against the Gibeonites.

ii. This promise from Deuteronomy 21:23 explains why Jesus died the way He did. Galatians 3:13 explains: *Christ has redeemed us from the curse of the law, having become a curse for us (for it is written, "Cursed is everyone who hangs on a tree").*

5. (10-14a) Rizpah's vigil.

Now Rizpah the daughter of Aiah took sackcloth and spread it for herself on the rock, from the beginning of harvest until the late rains poured on them from heaven. And she did not allow the birds of the air to rest on them by day nor the beasts of the field by night. And David was told what Rizpah the daughter of Aiah, the concubine of Saul, had done. Then David went and took the bones of Saul, and the bones of Jonathan his son, from the men of Jabesh Gilead who had stolen them from the street of Beth Shan, where the Philistines had hung them up, after the Philistines had struck down Saul in Gilboa. So he brought up the bones of Saul and the bones of Jonathan his son from there; and they gathered the bones of those who had been hanged. They buried the bones of Saul and Jonathan his son in the country of Benjamin in Zelah, in the tomb of Kish his father.

a. **Spread it for herself on the rock... until the late rains poured on them from heaven**: Rizpah - the mother of two of the seven delivered for execution - held a vigil over the bodies until the **late rains** came. The coming of rain showed that the famine was over, that justice was satisfied, and that Israel was delivered.

i. This means that the bodies of these men were deliberately left unburied. This was to emphasize the fact that these men were executed as an act of judgment.

b. **They gathered the bones**: David gave these seven a public burial, together with the remains of Saul and Jonathan.

6. (14b) The famine ends.

So they performed all that the king commanded. And after that God heeded the prayer for the land.

a. **They performed all that the king commanded**: David directed all of this and he did it partly on the principle stated in Numbers 35:33: *So you shall not pollute the land where you are; for blood defiles the land, and no atonement can be made for the land, for the blood that is shed on it, except by the blood of him who shed it.* The idea is that blood from unpunished murders defiles a land and God will one day require that blood from the nation.

b. **After that God heeded the prayer for the land**: It wasn't as if from the time Saul massacred the Gibeonites until David's day that God did not answer any of Israel's prayers. Yet there came a time when God wanted to deal with this sin, and at that time He would not answer their prayers until they dealt with it.

i. There are many reasons for unanswered prayer. When we see that our prayers are not answered we should seek God to address the problem.

B. Defeat of the Philistine giants.

1. (15-17) David retires from active duty.

When the Philistines were at war again with Israel, David and his servants with him went down and fought against the Philistines; and David grew faint. Then Ishbi-Benob, who *was* one of the sons of the giant, the weight of whose bronze spear *was* three hundred *shekels*, who was bearing a new *sword*, thought he could kill David. But Abishai the son of Zeruiah came to his aid, and struck the Philistine and killed him. Then the men of David swore to him, saying, "You shall go out no more with us to battle, lest you quench the lamp of Israel."

a. **And David grew faint**: Even a great man of God grows old. As the years went on, David became unable to fight as he once did. In this battle against the Philistines David's life was endangered when he **grew faint** in battle against a descendant of Goliath.

i. Israel faced the challenge of what they would do when they saw weakness in their leader. Since it was a weakness that could be understood - David's increasing frailty in old age - they should rally around their leader and supply what he cannot.

b. **Abishai the son of Zeruiah came to his aid**: When David's strength failed, God protected him through the strength of others. God will allow us to be in places where we need the strength of others.

> i. *Two are better than one, because they have a good reward for their labor. For if they fall, one will lift up his companion. But woe to him who is alone when he falls, for he has no one to help him up... Though one may be overpowered by another, two can withstand him.* (Ecclesiastes 4:9-12)

c. **You shall go out no more with us to battle**: In his advanced age, it was time for David to retire from the field of battle. His season as a warrior had passed.

> i. "David is considered as the *lamp* by which all Israel was guided, and without whom all the nation must be involved in darkness." (Clarke)

> ii. "The body drowneth not whilst the head is above water; when that once sinketh, death is near: so here. Pray therefore for the preservation of good princes; we cannot pray for them, and not pray for ourselves." (Trapp)

2. (18-22) Killing three more Philistine giants.

Now it happened afterward that there was again a battle with the Philistines at Gob. Then Sibbechai the Hushathite killed Saph, who *was* one of the sons of the giant. Again there was war at Gob with the Philistines, where Elhanan the son of Jaare-Oregim the Bethlehemite killed *the brother of* Goliath the Gittite, the shaft of whose spear *was* like a weaver's beam. Yet again there was war at Gath, where there was a man of *great* stature, who had six fingers on each hand and six toes on each foot, twenty-four in number; and he also was born to the giant. So when he defied Israel, Jonathan the son of Shimea, David's brother, killed him. These four were born to the giant in Gath, and fell by the hand of David and by the hand of his servants.

a. **Now it happened afterward**: This description of victory over Philistine giants showed that Israel could slay giants without David.

> i. **Sibbechai... Elhanan... Jonathan**: These men accomplished heroic deeds when David was finished fighting giants. God will continue to raise up leaders when the leaders of the previous generation pass from the scene.

> ii. David's legacy lay not only in what he accomplished, but also in what he left behind - a people prepared for victory. David's triumphs

were meaningful not only for himself but for others who learned victory through his teaching and example.

b. **Who had six fingers on each hand and six toes on each foot**: Commentators like Adam Clarke can't resist reminding us that this is a known phenomenon. "This is not a solitary instance: *Tavernier* informs us that the eldest son of the emperor of Java, who reigned in 1649, had *six fingers* on each hand, and *six toes* on each foot... I once saw a young girl, in the county of Londonderry, in Ireland, who had six fingers on each hand, and six toes on each foot, but her stature had nothing gigantic in it."

c. **Fell by the hand of David and by the hand of his servants**: Part of the idea is that David conquers enemies in the present, so it will be better for Solomon in the future. Our present victory is not only good for us now, but it also passes something important on to the next generation.

i. The defeat of these four giants is rightly credited to **the hand of David** *and* **the hand of his servants**. David had a role in this through his example, his guidance, and his influence.

ii. "Let those who after long service find themselves waning in strength, be content to abide with the people of god, still shining for them as a lamp, and thus enabling them to carry on the same Divine enterprises. Such action in the last days of life is also great and high service." (Morgan)

2 Samuel 22 - David's Psalm of Praise

A. Part One: Praise, Deliverance, and the Reason for Deliverance.

1. (1) Introduction to the psalm.

Then David spoke to the LORD the words of this song, on the day when the LORD had delivered him from the hand of all his enemies, and from the hand of Saul.

a. **Then David spoke to the LORD the words of this song**: For many reasons, most commentators assume that this was a psalm David wrote and sung many years before and is inserted at the end of 2 Samuel out of its chronological place. This is possible, but not necessary.

i. "The psalm appears almost as David's final words. Hence, it is a summary thanksgiving for God's many deliverances of him through his long life of service." (Boice)

b. **The words of this song**: With minor variations, this psalm is the same as Psalm 18. It is likely that David composed this song as a younger man - perhaps when Saul died, and he first took the throne, as described in 2 Samuel 8:14, when David had subdued all his enemies, *and the LORD preserved David wherever he went.* Yet in his old age David could look back with great gratitude and sing this song *again*, looking at his whole life.

i. This psalm is a great summary of David's whole character and attitude through life. "Such convictions - of the absolute sovereignty of Jehovah, of His omnipotent power to deliver, of the necessity for obedience to His law, and of assurance that in the case of such obedience He ever acts for His people - constituted the underlying strength of David's character." (Morgan)

ii. "We have another form of this Psalm with significant variations. . . and this suggests the idea that it was sung by David at different times when he reviewed his own remarkable history, and observed the gracious hand of God in it all." (Spurgeon)

2. (2-4) David praises the God of his deliverance.

And he said:
"The LORD *is* my rock and my fortress and my deliverer;
The God of my strength, in whom I will trust;
My shield and the horn of my salvation,
My stronghold and my refuge;
My Savior, You save me from violence.
I will call upon the LORD, *who is worthy* to be praised;
So shall I be saved from my enemies.

a. **My rock and my fortress and my deliverer**: David piled title upon title in praising God. God's work for David was so big and comprehensive that it couldn't be contained in one title.

   i. "In the opening sentence, which we have emphasized, the sense of truth is reinforced by the final words, '*even mine.*' By them the singer revealed the fact that all he celebrated in son was more than theory, it was experience." (Morgan)

   ii. David *experienced* the LORD's deliverance:

   • God delivered David from Goliath.

   • God delivered David from Saul.

   • God delivered David from backsliding.

   • God delivered David from Israel's enemies.

   • God delivered David from Absalom.

   • God delivered David from David's own sinful passions.

b. **In whom I will trust**: When we see God for who He is, it is easy to **trust** Him. When we know He is our **rock** and **fortress** and **deliverer** and **shield** and **stronghold** and **Savior**, it is natural to then **trust** Him completely.

   i. Faith does not completely depend on knowledge, but the right knowledge of God gives great strength to faith.

c. **My Savior, You save me**: Each title was meaningful to David because God fulfilled the meaning of each title in David's experience. This isn't a list of the names of God one might find in a systematic theology; this is the knowledge of God combined with the right experience of God.

d. **I will call upon the LORD, who is worthy to be praised**: "It is well to pray to God as to one who deserves to be praised, for then we plead in a happy and confident manner. If I feel that I can and do bless the Lord for all his past goodness, I am bold to ask great things of him." (Spurgeon)

3. (5-20) David's deliverance comes from God.

"When the waves of death surrounded me,
The floods of ungodliness made me afraid.
The sorrows of Sheol surrounded me;
The snares of death confronted me.
In my distress I called upon the LORD,
And cried out to my God;
He heard my voice from His temple,
And my cry *entered* His ears.
"Then the earth shook and trembled;
The foundations of heaven quaked and were shaken,
Because He was angry.
Smoke went up from His nostrils,
And devouring fire from His mouth;
Coals were kindled by it.
He bowed the heavens also, and came down
With darkness under His feet.
He rode upon a cherub, and flew;
And He was seen upon the wings of the wind.
He made darkness canopies around Him,
Dark waters *and* thick clouds of the skies.
From the brightness before Him
Coals of fire were kindled.
"The LORD thundered from heaven,
And the Most High uttered His voice.
He sent out arrows and scattered them;
Lightning bolts, and He vanquished them.
Then the channels of the sea were seen,
The foundations of the world were uncovered,
At the rebuke of the LORD,
At the blast of the breath of His nostrils.
"He sent from above, He took me,
He drew me out of many waters.
He delivered me from my strong enemy,
From those who hated me;
For they were too strong for me.
They confronted me in the day of my calamity,
But the LORD was my support.
He also brought me out into a broad place;
He delivered me because He delighted in me.

a. **Waves... floods... sorrows... snares**: Danger surrounded David on every side - physically, spiritually, emotionally, socially - David was on the brink of ruin when he cried out to God.

b. **In my distress I called upon the LORD**: The enemy of our soul wants us to believe that we can't call upon the LORD in our **distress** - as if we had to be right with God and sitting peacefully in a prayer chapel to pray rightly. David knew that God hears our **distress** signals.

c. **He heard my voice**: For David it was that simple. He cried out to God, and God **heard**. David also knew that God could not *hear* the distress of His people without taking action on their behalf.

d. **Then the earth shook**: God was so concerned about David's problem that it seemed to David as if He shook the earth to meet his need.

   i. "What is most impressive... is the magnificent way the psalmist describes God rising from his throne in heaven in response to his servant's cry, parting the clouds, and descending to fight the king's battles accompanied by earthquakes, thunder, storms, and lightning." (Boice)

e. **He rode upon a cherub, and flew**: David pictured the LORD coming to meet his need, coming with glory and speed. He came so fast to David that it seemed that God traveled **upon the wings of the wind**.

   i. "In the *original* of this sublime passage, *sense* and *sound* are astonishingly well connected... The *clap* of the *wing*, the *agitation* and *rush* through the air are expressed here in a very extraordinary manner." (Clarke)

f. **The Most High uttered His voice**: When God came He spoke up on David's behalf, commanding all creation to respond to His passionate desire to deliver His child.

   i. All this is a reflection of David's confidence in the love of God. David sees a God so loving that he won't tolerate the distress of His beloved. When things aren't right for His beloved all creation will see His passion and urgency to meet the need of His beloved.

g. **He took me... He drew me... He delivered me**: David saw God apply all that majesty and strength to the meeting of his need.

h. **They were too strong for me... the LORD was my support**: David knew that the victory was due to God's hand, not due to his own ingenuity or ability. Without the LORD for **support** David would fall.

i. **He delivered me because He delighted in me**: David had a sense of God's *delight* in him. His plea for deliverance was rooted in relationship, not merely in a desire to survive.

4. (21-25) Why God delivered David.

"The LORD rewarded me according to my righteousness;
According to the cleanness of my hands
He has recompensed me.
For I have kept the ways of the LORD,
And have not wickedly departed from my God.
For all His judgments *were* before me;
And *as for* His statutes, I did not depart from them.
I was also blameless before Him,
And I kept myself from my iniquity.
Therefore the LORD has recompensed me according to my
righteousness,
According to my cleanness in His eyes.

a. **According to the cleanness of my hands**: These words are one reason why many believe David could only sing this psalm *before* his sin with Bathsheba. Yet the text seems to indicate that David sang this towards the *end* of his days (2 Samuel 22:1).

i. We might say that David simply believed what the Prophet Nathan told him in 2 Samuel 12:13: *The LORD also has put away your sin*. David knew he was a forgiven man, and that the **cleanness of** his **hands** was because God cleansed them, not because they had never been dirtied.

ii. "If we were to remind David of his sin with Bathsheba, he would claim it as an illustration and a proof of this principle since he suffered in a variety of ways as a consequence of that great sin. But even though that happened, just as similar transgressions are committed by us all, on the whole he was nevertheless a man after God's own heart and was greatly blessed by God." (Boice)

b. **I have kept the ways of the LORD... I was also blameless before Him**: David isn't claiming sinless perfection. He spoke of his general righteousness and of his righteousness as it contrasted with the wickedness of his enemies.

i. "Before God the man after God's own heart was a humble sinner, but before his slanderers he could with unblushing face speak of the '*cleanness of his hands*' and the righteousness of his life." (Spurgeon)

ii. We can come to God in prayer with the same claim, but not on the basis of our own righteousness, but the righteousness we have *received* in Jesus (1 Corinthians 1:30 and 2 Corinthians 5:21).

c. **I kept myself from my iniquity**: Some think this is arrogance or pride on David's part. Spurgeon quotes one commentator who wrote, "Kept himself! Who made man his own keeper?" Yet we know there is certainly a sense in which we must keep ourselves from sin, even as Paul spoke of a man cleansing himself for God's glory and for greater service (2 Timothy 2:21).

B. Part Two: The Reason for Deliverance, Deliverance, and Praise.

1. (26-30) Why God delivered David.

"With the merciful You will show Yourself merciful;
With a blameless man You will show Yourself blameless;
With the pure You will show Yourself pure;
And with the devious You will show Yourself shrewd.
You will save the humble people;
But Your eyes *are* on the haughty, *that* You may bring *them* down.
"For You *are* my lamp, O LORD;
The LORD shall enlighten my darkness.
For by You I can run against a troop;
By my God I can leap over a wall.

a. **With the merciful You will show Yourself merciful**: Jesus discussed this principle in the sermon on the mount but from the perspective of man instead of from God: *For with what judgment you judge, you will be judged; and with the measure you use, it will be measured back to you.* (Matthew 7:2)

i. "In these words we have revealed the principles of relationship between God and man. God is to man what man is to God." (Morgan)

ii. David didn't only *sing* about this principle; he also lived it and benefited from it. God showed David great mercy because he showed great mercy to others, like Saul (1 Samuel 24:10-13) and Shimei (2 Samuel 16:7-12).

iii. "Note that even the merciful need mercy; no amount of generosity to the poor, or forgiveness to enemies, can set us beyond the need of mercy." (Spurgeon)

b. **With the devious You will show Yourself shrewd**: Translators have trouble with this sentence because it communicates a difficult concept. It's easy to say that if a man is pure towards God then God will be pure to him. But you can't say that if a man is wicked towards God then God will be wicked towards him, because God can't do anything wicked.

i. "David expresses the second half of the parallel by a somewhat ambiguous word, the root meaning of which is 'twisted.' The verse actually says, 'To the twisted (or crooked) you will show yourself twisted (or crooked)'... The idea seems to be that if a person insists in going devious ways in his dealings with God, God will outwit him, as that man deserves." (Boice)

c. **You will save the humble people; but Your eyes are on the haughty, that You may bring them down**: David proclaims his confidence in the principle repeated in Proverbs 3:34, James 4:6, and 1 Peter 5:5: *God resists the proud, but gives grace to the humble.*

i. There is something in true humility that prompts the grace and mercy of God and there is something in pride and haughtiness that prompts his resistance and displeasure.

ii. Humility isn't necessarily a *low* opinion of self; it is a combination of *accurate* opinion of self and simple self-forgetfulness. Humility is *others*-centered not *self*-centered.

d. **The LORD shall enlighten my darkness**: When God met David's need He first brought *light*. Great strength and skill don't help much at all if we can't *see* in the midst of the struggle.

e. **By You I can run against a troop; by my God I can leap over a wall**: When God met David's need He brought *strength*. One man should not be able to battle **a troop**, nor should he be able to **leap over a wall** protecting a city.

i. David knew the principle of Ephesians 6:10 long before Paul penned the words: *Be strong in the Lord and in the power of His might.* God has a resource of power (*His might*) that He makes available to us by faith. We don't have to be strong in *our* might, but we can be strong in *His might.*

2. (31-46) David's deliverance comes from God.

As for **God, His way *is* perfect;**
The word of the LORD *is* proven;
He *is* a shield to all who trust in Him.
"For who *is* God, except the LORD?
And who *is* a rock, except our God?
God *is* my strength *and* power,
And He makes my way perfect.
He makes my feet like the *feet* of deer,
And sets me on my high places.
He teaches my hands to make war,

So that my arms can bend a bow of bronze.
"You have also given me the shield of Your salvation;
Your gentleness has made me great.
You enlarged my path under me;
So my feet did not slip.
"I have pursued my enemies and destroyed them;
Neither did I turn back again till they were destroyed.
And I have destroyed them and wounded them,
So that they could not rise;
They have fallen under my feet.
For You have armed me with strength for the battle;
You have subdued under me those who rose against me.
You have also given me the necks of my enemies,
So that I destroyed those who hated me.
They looked, but *there was* none to save;
Even to the Lord, but He did not answer them.
Then I beat them as fine as the dust of the earth;
I trod them like dirt in the streets,
And I spread them out.
"You have also delivered me from the strivings of my people;
You have kept me as the head of the nations.
A people I have not known shall serve me.
The foreigners submit to me;
As soon as they hear, they obey me.
The foreigners fade away,
And come frightened from their hideouts.

a. **He is a shield to all who trust in Him**: When God met David's need He brought *protection*. David could see with light and stand in God's strength, but he still needed supernatural protection. David's **trust** was the vital link in receiving this protection from God.

b. **He makes my feet like the feet of deer, and sets me on my high places**: David thought of how the **deer** seem to skip from place to place and never lose their footing. God gave him the same kind of skill in working through the challenges brought by his enemies.

c. **So that my arms can bend a bow of bronze**: David thought of the strength needed to bend a bow made **of bronze**. God gave him the same kind of strength to overcome the challenges brought by his enemies.

d. **Your gentleness has made me great**: For David, it wasn't only about skill and power. It was also about receiving God's mercy and enjoying relationship with the God of great **gentleness**. This also was a resource of strength for David.

> i. "We might brave the lion; we are vanquished by the Lamb. We could withstand the scathing look of scorn; but when the gentle Lord casts on us the look of ineffable tenderness, we go out to weep bitterly." (Meyer)

e. **I have pursued my enemies and destroyed them**: David relished the place of *victory* he had in the LORD. He wasn't hesitant to proclaim it, either out of false humility or out of uncertainty of possessing the victory. He knew that enemies might rise again, but he looked back at the field of battle and said, "**They have fallen under my feet**, and when they were under my feet **I trod them like dirt in the streets**."

f. **You have also delivered me from the strivings of my people**: David didn't only have to battle with problems from enemies, but also with **the strivings** of his own **people**. In the midst of the battle he had to endure the contention of his own people, but God sustained him through that also.

g. **You have kept me as the head of the nations**: David knew that the throne belonged to God. David knew, "The throne is not mine. Not to have, not to take, not to protect, and not to keep. The throne is the LORD's." Therefore, when David *had* the throne, he knew it was *God* who gave it to him.

3. (47-51) David praises the God of his deliverance.

"The LORD lives!
Blessed *be* my Rock!
Let God be exalted,
The Rock of my salvation!
***It is* God who avenges me,**
And subdues the peoples under me;
He delivers me from my enemies.
You also lift me up above those who rise against me;
You have delivered me from the violent man.
Therefore I will give thanks to You, O LORD, among the Gentiles,
And sing praises to Your name.
"*He is* the tower of salvation to His king,
And shows mercy to His anointed,
To David and his descendants forevermore."

a. **The LORD lives! Blessed be my Rock**: David thought of the great victory of God on his behalf and could only worship.

b. **It is God who avenges me, and subdues the peoples under me**: David emphasized the thought, "This is the LORD's victory. He won it for me. The glory goes to Him."

c. **He delivers me from my enemies. You also lift me up**: We see in this psalm that David constantly moved back and forth from speaking *about* God (**He delivers me**) to speaking directly *to* God (**You also lift me up**). David didn't seem to have a problem moving between the two aspects, indicating that there is place for both in praise.

d. **And sing praises to Your name**: "To be saved singing is to be saved indeed. Many are saved mourning and doubting; but David had such faith that he could fight singing, and with the battle with a song still on his lips." (Spurgeon)

    i. Paul quotes 2 Samuel 22:50 (Psalm 18:49) in Romans 15:9.

e. **And shows mercy to His anointed**: David ended the psalm understanding his position in **mercy**. Though earlier in the psalm he proclaimed his own righteousness, he came back to the foundation of God's **mercy**. David's relationship with God was based on God's great **mercy**, not upon David's own righteousness.

2 Samuel 23 - David's Last Psalm

A. David's last psalm.

1. (1-4) The character of God's perfect king.

Now these *are* the last words of David.

***Thus* says David the son of Jesse;**
***Thus* says the man raised up on high,**
The anointed of the God of Jacob,
And the sweet psalmist of Israel:
"The Spirit of the LORD spoke by me,
And His word *was* on my tongue.
The God of Israel said,
The Rock of Israel spoke to me:
'He who rules over men *must be* just,
Ruling in the fear of God.
And *he shall be* like the light of the morning *when* the sun rises,
A morning without clouds,
***Like* the tender grass *springing* out of the earth,**
By clear shining after rain.'

> a. **These are the last words of David**: It wasn't that these were the words David spoke from his deathbed, but they expressed his heart and longing at the end of his life.

>> i. "I suppose the *last poetical composition* is here intended. He might have spoken many words after these in *prose*, but none in *verse*." (Clarke)

>> ii. This short psalm is a beautiful song of wisdom from David at the end of his life. "Wherein he doth, in few words but full of matter, acknowledge God's benefits, confess his sins, profess his faith, comfort

himself in the covenant, and denounce destruction to unbelievers... How much in a little!" (Trapp)

iii. What a life his was - we have a capsule of David's life in the titles and descriptions of 2 Samuel 23:1:

- **The son of Jesse**: Jesse was a humble farmer and this title reminds us of David's humble beginning.

- **The man raised up on high**: David allowed *God* to raise him up, so that he could confidently rest in this title.

- **The anointed of the God of Jacob**: David was **anointed** by God, not by himself or merely by man. He had a unique empowering and enabling from God.

- **The sweet psalmist of Israel**: David had a beautiful gift of eloquence and expression before God. This title reminds of David's deep inner life with God.

b. **The Spirit of the LORD spoke by me**: This indicates that at least at times, David was aware of the work of divine inspiration through him and expressed in his words.

c. **He who rules over men must be just**: As David looked back over his life and reign, he was struck by the great need for rulers to exercise *justice*. He knew this by seeing the goodness of justice provided and the curse of justice denied.

d. **Ruling in the fear of God**: This is the key to *justice* in the work of a leader. When leaders rule **in the fear of God** they recognize that a God of justice reviews their work and will require an accounting of how the ruler has led.

e. **He shall be like the light of the morning**: David reflected on how a wise ruler is blessed when he rules with justice. Though David's reign was not perfect it was blessed - and his reign is the most identified with the reign of the Messiah.

i. From one perspective David's reign was a disaster. He suffered from a dark scandal during his reign, he suffered under repeated family crises, under an attempted insurrection from his own son, under another civil war, and from three years of famine.

ii. In contrast to David, his son Solomon's reign seemed perfect. Solomon enjoyed a reign of peace, great prosperity, prominence, and glory.

iii. Yet the Bible has nothing but praise for David and his reign, reflected in passages like Psalm 89:20, Isaiah 55:3-4, Romans 1:3, and

Revelation 22:16. In contrast, Solomon is barely mentioned in the rest of the Scriptures and when he is, it is almost in a backhanded way (see Matthew 6:28-29 and Matthew 12:42).

iv. The difference between David and Solomon was found in their different relationships with God. David's passion in life was simply to be with God (Psalm 84:10), while Solomon's passion was personal improvement (1 Kings 3:4-15). We can also say that David endured to the end, loving and serving God in the final chapters of his life (2 Samuel 23:1-7), while Solomon forsook God in his later years (1 Kings 11:4-8).

2. (5-7) David's trust in God's covenant.

"Although my house *is* not so with God,
Yet He has made with me an everlasting covenant,
Ordered in all *things* and secure.
For *this is* all my salvation and all *my* desire;
Will He not make *it* increase?
But *the sons* of rebellion *shall* all *be* as thorns thrust away,
Because they cannot be taken with hands.
But the man *who* touches them
Must be armed with iron and the shaft of a spear,
And they shall be utterly burned with fire in *their* place."

a. **Although my house is not so with God**: David looked at the complete blessedness of a just ruler's reign and he knew that his reign fell short of both perfect justice and complete blessedness.

b. **Yet He has made with me an everlasting covenant**: David knew that the **everlasting covenant** from God was not based on David's perfection as a ruler. It was based on God's gracious commitment to His **everlasting covenant**.

c. **This is all my salvation and all my desire**: David only said this because the covenant was based on God's faithfulness and not his own. David knew that his own obedience was not enough to be a foundation for all his **salvation** and all his **desire**.

i. We can say that because of his sin and its consequences, David's light dimmed towards the end of his life, but it was not extinguished. He shined until the end. "In the Divine dealing with us, there is no mistake, no lapse. Nothing has been permitted which has not been made to serve the highest purpose. This is so even of our failures, if, like David, in true penitence we have forsaken them and confessed them. It is certainly so of all our sorrows and trials." (Morgan)

d. **The sons of rebellion shall all be as thorns thrust away**: The covenant was based on God's faithfulness, but David knew that obedience still mattered. God would still oppose **the sons of rebellion** and they would end in ruin. David knew he could trust the LORD to take care of his enemies and wicked men.

i. "This was the whole theme of David. The Lord is in control. Rest in Him. Don't fret yourself because of the evildoers that bring evil devices to pass. Rest in the Lord, trust also in Him. Delight thyself in the Lord! And all of the help, and the strength, the ministry of God's Spirit to our hearts, through the Psalms, the sweet psalmist of Israel. What a legacy he has left." (Smith)

ii. This remarkable relationship with God is the reason why David was Israel's greatest king, and the most prominent ancestor of Jesus Christ. The New Testament begins with these words: *The book of the genealogy of Jesus Christ, the Son of David* (Matthew 1:1).

B. David's mighty men.

1. (8-12) The names and exploits of David's top three soldiers.

These *are* the names of the mighty men whom David had: Josheb-Basshebeth the Tachmonite, chief among the captains. He was called Adino the Eznite, because he had killed eight hundred men at one time. And after him *was* Eleazar the son of Dodo, the Ahohite, *one* of the three mighty men with David when they defied the Philistines *who* were gathered there for battle, and the men of Israel had retreated. He arose and attacked the Philistines until his hand was weary, and his hand stuck to the sword. The LORD brought about a great victory that day; and the people returned after him only to plunder. And after him *was* Shammah the son of Agee the Hararite. The Philistines had gathered together into a troop where there was a piece of ground full of lentils. Then the people fled from the Philistines. But he stationed himself in the middle of the field, defended it, and killed the Philistines. And the LORD brought about a great victory.

a. **These are the names of the mighty men**: David was nothing without his mighty men, and they were nothing without him. He was their leader, but a leader is nothing without followers - and David had **the mighty men** to follow him. These men didn't necessarily *start* as mighty men; many were some of the distressed, indebted, and discontent people who followed David at Adullam Cave (1 Samuel 22:1-2).

i. "These men came to David when his fortunes were at the lowest ebb, and he himself was regarded as a rebel and an outlaw, and they remained faithful to him throughout their lives. Happy are they who can follow a good cause in its worst estate, for theirs is true glory." (Spurgeon)

ii. The day for mighty men and women - heroic men and women for God - has not ended. "The triumph of the church as a whole depends upon the personal victory of every Christian. In other words, your victory, your life, your personal testimony, are important to the cause of God today. What happens out in New Guinea, down in the Amazon jungle, over in disturbed Congo, is not unrelated to what happens in your own personal relationship with God and your personal battle against the forces of darkness. Victory for the church on the whole world-front depends upon victory in your life and in mine; 'home' and 'foreign' situations cannot be detached." (Redpath)

b. **Adino the Eznite**: This leader among David's mighty men was noted for having **killed eight hundred men at one time**.

i. "THREE *hundred* is the reading in Chronicles, and seems to be the true one." (Clarke)

c. **Eleazar the son of Dodo**: This leader of David's mighty men was famous for hanging with David in a famous battle and when his **hand was weary, and his hand stuck to the sword**. Through his tenacity **the LORD brought about a great victory that day**.

i. Spurgeon saw that Eleazar, in his solitary stand until victory, was a tremendous example for believers today. "Solitary prowess is expected of believers. I hope we may breed in this place a race of men and women who know the truth, and know also what the Lord claims at their hands, and are resolved, by the help of the Holy Spirit, to war a good warfare for their Lord whether others will stand at their side or no."

ii. "Remember Mr. Sankey's hymn, - 'Dare to be a Daniel! Dare to stand alone! Dare to have a purpose firm! Dare to make it known!' Dare to be an Eleazar, and go forth and smite the Philistines alone; you will soon find that there are others in the house who have concealed their sentiments, but when they see, you coming forward, they will be openly on the Lord's side. Many cowards are skulking about, try to shame them. Many are undecided, let them see a brave man, and he will be the standard-bearer around whom they will rally." (Spurgeon)

d. **Shammah the son of Agee the Hararite**: This leader among David's mighty men **stationed himself in the middle of the field** when others fled, and he held the ground single-handedly until the LORD **brought about a great victory**.

2. (13-17) A daring exploit from David's days at Adullam.

Then three of the thirty chief men went down at harvest time and came to David at the cave of Adullam. And the troop of Philistines encamped in the Valley of Rephaim. David *was* **then in the stronghold, and the garrison of the Philistines** *was* **then** *in* **Bethlehem. And David said with longing, "Oh, that someone would give me a drink of the water from the well of Bethlehem, which** *is* **by the gate!" So the three mighty men broke through the camp of the Philistines, drew water from the well of Bethlehem that** *was* **by the gate, and took it and brought** *it* **to David. Nevertheless he would not drink it, but poured it out to the LORD. And he said, "Far be it from me, O LORD, that I should do this! Is** *this not* **the blood of the men who went in** *jeopardy of* **their lives?" Therefore he would not drink it. These things were done by the three mighty men.**

a. **Came to David at the cave of Adullam**: David spent time in this cave when those who would become his mighty men first came to him in 1 Samuel 22:1-2. This passage describes something that happened either during that time or a later time of battle against the Philistines when David went back to **the cave of Adullam**.

b. **David said with longing, "Oh, that someone would give me a drink of the water from the well of Bethlehem"**: During this time David had a nostalgic longing for the taste of water from a well near his boyhood home.

c. **The three mighty men broke through the camp of the Philistines, drew water from the well of Bethlehem**: In response to David's longing - which wasn't a command or even a request, just a vocalized longing - these **three mighty men** immediately went to fulfill David's desire at great personal risk.

d. **He would not drink it, but poured it out to the LORD**: David was so honored by the self-sacrifice of these three mighty men he felt that the water was too good for him - and worthy to be **poured** out in sacrifice to the LORD. He believed that the great sacrifice of these men could only be honored by giving the water to the LORD.

i. "Accounting it too dear a draught for himself, he poured it out unto the Lord, out of a religious respect." (Trapp)

3. (18-23) Two more notable men among the mighty men.

Now Abishai the brother of Joab, the son of Zeruiah, was chief of *another* **three. He lifted his spear against three hundred** *men,* **killed** *them,* **and won a name among** *these* **three. Was he not the most honored of three?**

Therefore he became their captain. However, he did not attain to the *first* three. Benaiah *was* the son of Jehoiada, the son of a valiant man from Kabzeel, who had done many deeds. He had killed two lion-like heroes of Moab. He also had gone down and killed a lion in the midst of a pit on a snowy day. And he killed an Egyptian, a spectacular man. The Egyptian *had* a spear in his hand; so he went down to him with a staff, wrested the spear out of the Egyptian's hand, and killed him with his own spear. These *things* Benaiah the son of Jehoiada did, and won a name among three mighty men. He was more honored than the thirty, but he did not attain to the *first* three. And David appointed him over his guard.

> a. **Abishai the brother of Joab**: This leader among David's mighty men was famous for his battle against **three hundred men**. His leadership is also recorded in passages like 1 Samuel 26:6-9, 2 Samuel 3:30, and 2 Samuel 10:10-14.

> b. **Benaiah the son of Jehoiada**: This leader among David's mighty men was famous for his battles against both men (**two lion-like heroes of Moab... an Egyptian, a spectacular man**) and beasts (**a lion in the midst of a pit on a snowy day**).

4. (24-39) A list of David's mighty men.

Asahel the brother of Joab *was* one of the thirty; Elhanan the son of Dodo of Bethlehem, Shammah the Harodite, Elika the Harodite, Helez the Paltite, Ira the son of Ikkesh the Tekoite, Abiezer the Anathothite, Mebunnai the Hushathite, Zalmon the Ahohite, Maharai the Netophathite, Heleb the son of Baanah (the Netophathite), Ittai the son of Ribai from Gibeah of the children of Benjamin, Benaiah a Pirathonite, Hiddai from the brooks of Gaash, Abi-Albon the Arbathite, Azmaveth the Barhumite, Eliahba the Shaalbonite (of the sons of Jashen), Jonathan, Shammah the Hararite, Ahiam the son of Sharar the Hararite, Eliphelet the son of Ahasbai, the son of the Maachathite, Eliam the son of Ahithophel the Gilonite, Hezrai the Carmelite, Paarai the Arbite, Igal the son of Nathan of Zobah, Bani the Gadite, Zelek the Ammonite, Naharai the Beerothite (armorbearer of Joab the son of Zeruiah), Ira the Ithrite, Gareb the Ithrite, *and* Uriah the Hittite: thirty-seven in all.

> a. **Eliam the son of Ahithophel**: This man is notable among the mighty men because he was the father of Bathsheba (2 Samuel 3:11) and shows that Ahithophel was Bathsheba's grandfather.

> b. **Uriah the Hittite**: He is notable among the mighty men because he was the husband of Bathsheba. When David heard of Bathsheba's relation

to **Uriah** and **Eliam** and **Ahithophel** (2 Samuel 3:11) he should have put away every idea of adultery.

c. **Thirty-seven in all**: These remarkable men were the foundation of the greatness of David's reign. They did not come to David as great men, but God used his leadership to transform them from men who were *in distress, in debt* and *discontented*, who met David back at Adullam Cave (1 Samuel 22:1-2).

> i. "More than all his victories against outside foes, the influence of his life and character on the men nearest to him testify to his essential greatness." (Morgan)

2 Samuel 24 - David and the Census

A. David commands a census to be taken.

1. (1-2) David is moved to take a census.

Again the anger of the LORD was aroused against Israel, and He moved David against them to say, "Go, number Israel and Judah." So the king said to Joab the commander of the army who *was* with him, "Now go throughout all the tribes of Israel, from Dan to Beersheba, and count the people, that I may know the number of the people."

a. **The anger of the LORD was aroused against Israel, and He moved David**: The translators of the New King James Version believe that "**He**" in this sentence applies to God, because they capitalize it. Yet 1 Chronicles 21:1 tells us, *Now Satan stood up against Israel, and moved David to number Israel.* The best explanation is that Satan prompted King David and is the "he" of 2 Samuel 24:1. Yet the LORD expressly allowed it as a chastisement against David.

i. "Now the 'he' there, we assume would be the Lord. But as we find out in 1 Chronicles, chapter one, it was Satan that moved David's heart, to the numbering of the people. So God opened the door, and allowed Satan to move in and tempt David." (Smith)

b. **Go, number Israel and Judah**: This was dangerous because of a principle stated in Exodus 30:12: *When you take the census of the children of Israel for their number, then every man shall give a ransom for himself to the LORD, when you number them, that there may be no plague among them when you number them.*

i. The principle of Exodus 30:12 speaks to *God's ownership of His people*. In the thinking of these ancient cultures, a man only had the right to count or number what belonged to him. Israel didn't belong to David; Israel belonged to God. It was up to the LORD to command a counting, and if David counted he should only do it at God's command and receiving ransom money to "atone" for the counting.

2. (3-4) Joab objects to the census.

And Joab said to the king, "Now may the Lord your God add to the people a hundred times more than there are, and may the eyes of my lord the king see *it*. But why does my lord the king desire this thing?" Nevertheless the king's word prevailed against Joab and against the captains of the army. Therefore Joab and the captains of the army went out from the presence of the king to count the people of Israel.

a. **Why does my lord the king desire this thing**: Joab wasn't afraid to speak to David when he thought the king was wrong. With the best interest of both David and Israel in mind, Joab tactfully asked David to reconsider this foolish desire to count the nation.

i. Joab also hinted at the *motive* behind the counting - pride in David. The **this thing** that David desired was the increase of the nation, and he perhaps wanted to measure the size of his army to know if he had enough force to conquer a neighboring nation. "He did it out of curiosity and creature-confidence." (Trapp)

ii. So late in his reign, David was tempted to take some of the glory in himself. He looked at how Israel had grown and prospered during his reign - it was remarkable indeed. The count was a way to take credit to himself. "The spirit of vainglory in numbers had taken possession of the people and the king, and there was a tendency to trust in numbers and forget God." (Morgan)

b. **Nevertheless the king's word prevailed against Joab and against the captains of the army**: It wasn't only Joab who tried to tell David not to do this - the **captains of the army** also warned David not to count the soldiers in Israel. But David did so anyway.

3. (5-9) The census is taken.

And they crossed over the Jordan and camped in Aroer, on the right side of the town which *is* in the midst of the ravine of Gad, and toward Jazer. Then they came to Gilead and to the land of Tahtim Hodshi; they came to Dan Jaan and around to Sidon; and they came to the stronghold of Tyre and to all the cities of the Hivites and the Canaanites. Then they went out to South Judah *as far as* Beersheba. So when they had gone through all the land, they came to Jerusalem at the end of nine months and twenty days. Then Joab gave the sum of the number of the people to the king. And there were in Israel eight hundred thousand valiant

men who drew the sword, and the men of Judah were five hundred thousand men.

a. **When they had gone through all the land**: It took almost 10 months to complete the census. David should have called off this foolish census during the 10 months, but he didn't.

b. **Joab gave the sum of the number of the people to the king**: The results showed that there were 1,300,000 fighting men among the twelve tribes, reflecting an estimated total population of about 6 million in Israel.

i. "In the parallel place, 1 Chronicles 21:5, the sums are widely different: in Israel *one million one hundred thousand*, in Judah *four hundred and seventy thousand*. Neither of these sums is too great, but they cannot be both correct; and which is the true number is difficult to say." (Clarke)

ii. "To attempt to reconcile them in every part is lost labour; better at once acknowledge what cannot be successfully denied, that although the original writers of the Old Testament wrote under the influence of the Divine Spirit, yet we are not told that the same influence descended on all *copiers* of their words, so as absolutely to prevent them from making mistakes." (Clarke)

B. David's guilt and God's punishment.

1. (10) David knows that he has done wrong in numbering the people.

And David's heart condemned him after he had numbered the people. So David said to the LORD, "I have sinned greatly in what I have done; but now, I pray, O LORD, take away the iniquity of Your servant, for I have done very foolishly."

a. **David's heart condemned him**: The man after God's heart was not sinless, but he had a heart sensitive to sin when it was committed. David kept a short account with God.

b. **Take away the iniquity of Your servant, for I have done very foolishly**: David now saw the pride and vainglory that prompted him to do such a foolish thing.

2. (11-13) David is allowed to choose his judgment.

Now when David arose in the morning, the word of the LORD came to the prophet Gad, David's seer, saying, "Go and tell David, 'Thus says the LORD: I offer you three *things;* choose one of them for yourself, that I may do *it* to you.'" So Gad came to David and told him; and he said to him, "Shall seven years of famine come to you in your land? Or shall you flee three months before your enemies, while they pursue you? Or

shall there be three days' plague in your land? Now consider and see what answer I should take back to Him who sent me."

a. **I offer you three things**: God used David's sin and the resulting chastisement to reveal David's heart and wisdom. His choice of the following three options were to test David:

- **Seven years of famine**: This would surely be the death of some in Israel, but the wealthy and resourceful would survive. Israel would have to depend on neighboring nations for food.

- **Flee three months before your enemies**: This would be the death of some in Israel, but mostly only of soldiers. Israel would have to contend with **enemies** among neighboring nations.

- **Three days' plague in your land**: This would be the death of some in Israel, but *anyone* could be struck by this plague - rich or poor, influential or anonymous, royalty or common.

b. **Now consider and see what answer I should take back to Him who sent me**: God wanted David to use the prophet as a mediator, and to answer to the prophet instead of directly to God.

3. (14) David chooses the three days of plague.

And David said to Gad, "I am in great distress. Please let us fall into the hand of the LORD, for His mercies *are* great; but do not let me fall into the hand of man."

a. **Please let me fall into the hand of the LORD**: This meant that David chose the three days of plague. In the other two options the king and his family could be insulated against the danger, but David knew that he had to expose *himself* to the chastisement of God.

i. "Had he chosen *war*, his own *personal safety* was in no danger, because there was already an ordinance preventing him from going to battle. Had he chosen *famine*, his own wealth would have secured his and his own family's support. But he showed the greatness of his mind in choosing the *pestilence*, to the ravages of which himself and his household were exposed equally with the meanest of his subjects." (Clarke)

b. **Do not let me fall into the hand of man**: This meant that David chose the three days of plague. In the other two options, Israel would either be at the mercy of neighbors (as in the famine) or attacked by enemies. David knew that God was far more merciful and gracious than man.

4. (15-17) The plague of destruction hits Israel severely.

So the LORD sent a plague upon Israel from the morning till the appointed time. From Dan to Beersheba seventy thousand men of the people died. And when the angel stretched out His hand over Jerusalem to destroy it, the LORD relented from the destruction, and said to the angel who was destroying the people, "It is enough; now restrain your hand." And the angel of the LORD was by the threshing floor of Araunah the Jebusite. Then David spoke to the LORD when he saw the angel who was striking the people, and said, "Surely I have sinned, and I have done wickedly; but these sheep, what have they done? Let Your hand, I pray, be against me and against my father's house."

a. **Seventy thousand men of the people died**: This was a great calamity upon Israel - a devastating plague striking so many in such a short period of time.

b. **The LORD relented from the destruction**: This justified David's wisdom in leaving himself in God's hands. He could not trust man to relent from destruction.

c. **Let Your hand, I pray, be against me and against my father's house**: Like a true shepherd, David asked that the punishment be upon him and his own household. Having another purpose to accomplish, God did not accept David's offer.

C. David builds an altar.

1. (18-21) David is instructed to erect an altar on the threshing floor of Araunah.

And Gad came that day to David and said to him, "Go up, erect an altar to the LORD on the threshing floor of Araunah the Jebusite." So David, according to the word of Gad, went up as the LORD commanded. Now Araunah looked, and saw the king and his servants coming toward him. So Araunah went out and bowed before the king with his face to the ground. Then Araunah said, "Why has my lord the king come to his servant?" And David said, "To buy the threshing floor from you, to build an altar to the LORD, that the plague may be withdrawn from the people."

a. **Erect an altar to the LORD on the threshing floor of Araunah the Jebusite**: This is where David met the Angel of the LORD, and where God relented from the plague before it came upon Jerusalem. Now God wanted David to meet Him there in worship.

i. "Threshing floors were usually on a height, in order to catch every breeze; some area to the north of David's city is indicated." (Baldwin)

ii. The **threshing floor of Araunah** had both a rich history and a rich future. 2 Chronicles 3:1 tells us that the threshing floor of Araunah was on Mount Moriah; the same hill where Abraham offered Isaac (Genesis 22:2), and the same set of hills where Jesus died on the cross (Genesis 22:14).

b. **To buy the threshing floor from you, to build an altar to the LORD:** David wanted to transform this place where chaff was separated from wheat into a place of sacrifice and worship. It would remain a place of sacrifice and worship because this land purchased by David became the site of Solomon's temple (1 Chronicles 21:28-22:5).

2. (22-24) Refusing the gift of Araunah, David *buys* the threshing floor.

Now Araunah said to David, "Let my lord the king take and offer up whatever *seems* good to him. Look, *here are* oxen for burnt sacrifice, and threshing implements and the yokes of the oxen for wood. All these, O king, Araunah has given to the king." And Araunah said to the king, "May the LORD your God accept you." Then the king said to Araunah, "No, but I will surely buy *it* from you for a price; nor will I offer burnt offerings to the LORD my God with that which costs me nothing." So David bought the threshing floor and the oxen for fifty shekels of silver.

a. **Let my lord the king take and offer up whatever seems good to him:** Araunah had a good, generous heart and wanted to *give* David anything he wanted.

i. "Had Araunah's noble offer been accepted, it would have been *Araunah's sacrifice*, not *David's*; nor would it have answered the end of turning away the displeasure of the Most High." (Clarke)

b. **I will surely buy it from you for a price; nor will I offer burnt offerings to the LORD my God with that which costs me nothing:** David knew that it would not be a *gift* nor a *sacrifice* unto the LORD if it did not cost him something. He didn't look for the cheapest way possible to please God.

i. "He who has a religion that *costs him nothing*, has a religion that is *worth nothing*: nor will any man esteem the ordinances of God, if those ordinances cost him nothing." (Clarke)

ii. "Where there is true, strong love to Jesus, it will cost us something. Love is the costliest of all undertakings... But what shall we mind if we gain Christ? You cannot give up for Him without regaining everything you have renounced, but purified and transfigured." (Meyer)

3. (25) David's altar and sacrifice.

And David built there an altar to the LORD, and offered burnt offerings and peace offerings. So the LORD heeded the prayers for the land, and the plague was withdrawn from Israel.

a. **And offered burnt offerings and peace offerings**: This shows that David understood that the death of the 70,000 in Israel in the plague did not *atone* for his and Israel's sin. Atonement could only be made through the blood of an approved substitute.

i. **Burnt offerings** were to atone for sin; **peace offerings** were to enjoy fellowship with God. This shows us from the beginning to the end, David's life was marked by fellowship with God.

ii. "We finally see the man after God's own heart turning the occasion of his sin and its punishment into an occasion of worship." (Morgan)

b. **So the LORD heeded the prayers for the land**: 1 Chronicles 21:26 tells us that God showed His acceptance of David's sacrifice by consuming it with fire from heaven. God honored David's desire to be right and to fellowship with God by answering with Divine blessing from heaven. So it always is when God's children draw near to their God and Father for cleansing and fellowship.

Bibliography - 2 Samuel

Baldwin, Joyce G. *1 and 2 Samuel, An Introduction and Commentary* (Leicester, England: Inter-Varsity Press, 1988)

Clarke, Adam *The Holy Bible, Containing the Old and New Testaments, with A Commentary and Critical Notes, Volume II – Joshua to Esther* (New York: Eaton and Mains, 1827?)

Cook, F.C. (Editor) *The Bible Commentary, 1 Samuel – Esther* (Grand Rapids, Michigan: Baker Book House, 1974)

Ellison, H.L. "Joshua - 2 Samuel," *Daily Bible Commentary, Volume 1: Genesis – Job* (London: Scripture Union, 1973)

Ginzberg, Louis *The Legends of the Jews, Volumes 1-7* (Philadelphia: The Jewish Publication Society of America, 1968)

Harris, R. Laid, Archer, Gleason L. Jr., and Waltke, Bruce K. *Theological Wordbook of the Old Testament* (Chicago: Moody Bible Institute, 1980)

Keil, C.F. and Delitszch, F. *Commentary on the Old Testament, Volume II – Joshua, Judges, Ruth, I & II Samuel* (Grand Rapids, Michigan: Eerdmans, 1984)

Maclaren, Alexander *Expostions of Holy Scripture, Volume 2* (Grand Rapids, Michigan: Baker Book House, 1984)

Meyer, F.B. *Our Daily Homily* (Westwood, New Jersey: Revell, 1966)

Meyer, F.B. *David: Shepherd, Psalmist, King* (Fort Washington, Pennsylvania: Christian Literature Crusade, 1977)

Morgan, G. Campbell Searchlights from the Word (New York: Revell, 1926)

Poole, Matthew *A Commentary on the Holy Bible, Volume 1* (London, Banner of Truth Trust, 1968)

Redpath, Alan *The Making of a Man of God – Studies in the Life of David* (Old Tappan, New Jersey: Revell, 1962)

Smith, R. Payne "1 Samuel," *The Pulpit Commentary, Volume 4 – Ruth, I & II Samuel* (McLean, Virginia: MacDonald Publishing, ?)

Spurgeon, Charles Haddon *The New Park Street Pulpit, Volumes 1-6* and *The Metropolitan Tabernacle Pulpit, Volumes 7-63* (Pasadena, Texas: Pilgrim Publications, 1990)

Trapp, John *A Commentary on the Old and New Testaments, Volume 1 – Genesis to Second Chronicles* (Eureka, California: Tanski Publications, 1997)

Youngblood, Ronald F. "1, 2 Samuel," *The Expositor's Bible Commentary, Volume 3* (Grand Rapids, Michigan: Zondervan, 1992)

As the years pass I love the work of studying, learning, and teaching the Bible more than ever. I'm so grateful that God is faithful to meet me in His Word.

Much thanks to the many who helped prepare this commentary. The year of this commentary's first publication (2004) was a year of change for our whole family, and my gratitude goes out to my wife Inga-Lill and our children who give so much support in this and all the ministry. Nathan - I really like the way that Nathan, the prophet and friend of David spoke the truth. It speaks to me of what you are and what you will be.

This book is the second time I received the proofreading help of Marrianne van de Vrede. It's a great gift to have a proofreader and editor who helps the writer learn more about writing. Thanks so much, Marrianne. Thanks to Brian Procedo for the cover design and all the graphics work.

Most especially, thanks to my wife Inga-Lill. She is my loved and valued partner in life and in service to God and His people.

David Guzik

David Guzik's Bible commentary is regularly used and trusted by many thousands who want to know the Bible better. Pastors, teachers, class leaders, and everyday Christians find his commentary helpful for their own understanding and explanation of the Bible. David and his wife Inga-Lill live in Santa Barbara, California.

You can email David at
david@enduringword.com

For more resources by David Guzik,
go to www.enduringword.com